Dinosaurs
for Kids

An Introduction to Dinosaur Paleontology

James Kuether

Dedication

For Jon

Acknowledgments

Great thanks to Professor Christopher Scotese for the generous use of his paleomaps.

Scotese, C.R., 2001. *Atlas of Earth History*, Volume 1, Paleogeography, PALEOMAP Project, Arlington, Texas, 52 pp. ResearchGate Academia.

Edited by Brett Ortler and Jenna Barron
Proofread by Emily Beaumont
Cover and book design by Jonathan Norberg

Cover photos: **aekky/Shutterstock:** dinosaur skin texture; **Rattana/Shutterstock:** child's hand

All images copyright by **James Kuether** unless otherwise noted.
Utah Geological Survey: 10
The following images used under license from **Shutterstock.com**:
aekky: 1 (dinosaur skin texture); **Alex Coan:** 8 (top); **Alona Siniehina:** 146; **Barks:** 5; **Bjoern Wylezich:** 8 (bottom); **Maderla:** 7; **paleontologist natural:** 6; **Romolo Tavani:** 30 (bottom); **Ryan M. Bolton:** 43 (both); and **TamaraLSanchez:** 13 (horse).

10 9 8 7 6 5 4 3 2 1
Dinosaurs for Kids: An Introduction to Dinosaur Paleontology
Copyright © 2024 by James Kuether
Published by Adventure Publications
An imprint of AdventureKEEN
310 Garfield Street South
Cambridge, Minnesota 55008
(800) 678-7006
www.adventurepublications.net
All rights reserved
Printed in the United States of America
LCCN 2023050375 (print); 2023050376 (ebook)
ISBN 978-1-64755-392-0 (pbk.); ISBN 978-1-64755-393-7 (ebook)

Table of Contents

Triceratops

Introduction

You've been surrounded by dinosaurs all your life. You see them everywhere you go. Toy shelves are filled with every dinosaur imaginable, and they star in the biggest blockbuster movies. You have probably been on school trips to museums where they are the star attractions, and you probably have at least one book about dinosaurs already on the shelf in your bedroom. If you do a Google search on the word *dinosaur*, you'll get over 57 million videos and 477 million web pages as results. Amazon offers over 20,000 dinosaur books and 30,000 dinosaur toys. You see them on T-shirts and hats, and they're featured on TV. Touring shows of robotic dinosaurs draw thousands when they come to town. Dinosaurs are *everywhere*.

And that's understandable because dinosaurs are just so amazing. Everyone is fascinated by them.

They were like real living monsters and there's nothing like them alive today.

But what do you really know about dinosaurs?

Dinosaurs are a group of reptiles that existed from about 230 million years ago until around 66 million years ago. At first, they were small and a minor part of their ecosystems. But before long, they became one of the most successful and dominant land animals to ever exist.

And we know this because, even though they lived millions of years ago, they left behind lots of clues about what they looked like and how they lived.

Fossils

The science of studying dinosaurs is called **paleontology,** and the scientists that practice it are called **paleontologists.** They rely on fossils to do most of their work. In fact, without fossils, we wouldn't know anything about dinosaurs. Fossils are the preserved remains of any once-living organism. Fossils

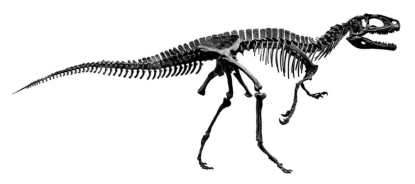

may be bones, footprints, skin impressions, or even **soft tissue**—actual skin, hair, or some other part of an animal preserved in amber.

FOSSILIZED BONES

When you go to the museum and see skeletons of dinosaurs, what you're seeing are not the actual bones of dinosaurs, but rather their **fossilized bones.** Even though it seems like there are a lot of dinosaur skeletons out there, fossilization is rare, and the conditions must be just right for it to occur. First, the dinosaur has to have died in an environment where its body could be covered in sediment—either sand or mud. Over time, minerals have seeped into the bones and turned them into rock. Hard body parts like bones and shells fossilize easier than soft body parts like skin and hair, which decay quickly after an animal dies. That's why most dinosaur fossils are of their bones.

Fossilized dinosaur bone

Fossilized bones are just one type of fossil that pale-ontologists use. A **trace fossil** preserves some record of an animal's activity, but not the preserved remains of the animal itself.

Fossil Footprints can be preserved when an animal has walked through sand or mud. These can tell us a great deal about an animal: how it stood and walked, how long its strides were, and even how fast it was moving. If footprints from several dinosaurs are preserved together, it could mean they moved in herds. Paleontologists have found preserved track-ways of predators chasing after prey. Some fossil footprints even show impressions of the dinosaur's skin, telling us if they had scaly feet or big foot pads.

Fossil dinosaur footprint

Fossilized Skin Impressions have been found for several dinosaurs, including duckbills, tyrannosaurs, and horned dinosaurs like *Triceratops*. Although these are usually small sections of skin, some are of large portions of the animal. We refer to these as "dinosaur mummies," though they're not made of actual mummified skin like Egyptian mummies. They're a cast of the skin left in the sediment after the dinosaur died. When the animal died, its body was covered in sediment (sand or mud). Over time, the sediment hardened, and the skin and other soft tissues decayed, leaving a cast or mold of the skin.

Coprolites are fossilized dinosaur poop. It sounds gross, but just like with fossilized bones, it's been turned into rock. By studying coprolites, we can get information about what a creature ate. Although we can't tell exactly which dinosaur it came from, we can make "best guesses" based on what dinosaurs are known from the area.

fossilized coprolite

Amber is petrified (hardened) tree resin, and although it's rare, it can provide amazing soft-tissue fossils. When an animal or some part of an animal, such as fur or feathers, gets stuck in the tree resin, it can fossilize over time, and the resin becomes hard.

amber containing an embedded insect

Fossilized insects are common, but we've also found feathers, hair, small lizards, and even a very tiny wing from a dinosaur, all preserved in amber.

Discovering Dinosaurs & Fossil Collecting

The bones and skeletons of dinosaurs you see in a museum are the result of hundreds of hours of hard work done by paleontologists.

Paleontologists find dinosaurs through **fieldwork.** This is when they go to areas where they've found dinosaur bones before or they think are likely to have bones. Once they've chosen a site, scientists can spend days, weeks, or even months looking around for signs of dinosaur fossils.

Usually, paleontologists will find tiny fragments of bone or teeth. These are signs that there may be more bones buried nearby. If they think the site looks promising, they carefully dig around the fragments they've found using small picks, shovels, and brushes to see if they can find more of the fossil.

Scientists use a great deal of care when they find a fossil. Their expertise allows them to determine how far they can safely dig and helps ensure they don't accidentally damage the fossil. Often, they'll only find a single bone. But on rare occasions, they find almost the entire animal.

There's always a lot of excitement when fragments of a dinosaur fossil are found in the field.

Once they've uncovered all of the fossil, it's wrapped in plaster bandages to protect it for transportation back to their laboratory. If the fossil is small, it may be carried off-site and transported in a truck. But if it's a large discovery, it may take major excavating equipment to remove and transport it.

Back in the laboratory, the slow and delicate process of removing the extra rock (called **matrix**) begins. The people who do this work are highly trained technicians called **fossil preparators,** and they use small tools like dental picks and tiny drills to expose the fossil bones. This process can take months, and even years.

Once the fossil is exposed, paleontologists begin the long process of analyzing and identifying the fossil, determining if it's a dinosaur that's already known or an entirely new species.

Digging dinosaurs is a long and difficult process that can involve dozens of experts over many years. Their knowledge and expertise ensure that dinosaur fossils are removed properly and safely.

FOSSIL COLLECTING

All this talk about fieldwork makes finding fossils sound like a lot of hard work, it's but also a lot of fun, and you may want to try your hand at it yourself!

Fossil collecting can be a fun and exciting hobby. There are many places around North America where certain fossils are common. Fossil shells—like those of snails and mollusks—are easy to find. Petrified wood is another kind of fossil that's common. All of these can be legally collected from many public lands.

But it's important to remember that collecting dinosaur fossils is against the law. Only professionals are allowed to dig and collect dinosaur fossils from public land. In fact, it's against the law to collect any vertebrate fossils. This includes fossils of fish, mammals, reptiles, amphibians, birds, and, yes, dinosaurs.

It's not very likely that you would find a dinosaur fossil, but if you do, don't touch it! You should notify authorities and let them know about the fossil. All dinosaur fossils are of great scientific interest, and it's important that they be properly collected and studied.

It's also important that you understand some of the rules around fossil collecting:

• Most national, state, and local parks forbid the collecting of fossils.

- It's against the law to collect fossils from Native American reservations.

- It's against the law to collect vertebrate fossils.

- If you're not sure if it's okay to collect fossils from a location, check with an adult.

- Never go fossil collecting alone! It's best to have an adult with you while fossil collecting. Many of the locations can be rugged and dangerous.

- Never go fossil collecting on private property unless you have permission from the land owner.

What Makes a Dinosaur a Dinosaur?

Dinosaurs didn't suddenly appear. Like all life on Earth, they evolved from primitive reptiles over millions and millions of years and through gradual physical changes and adaptations.

Dinosaurs have several distinct physical characteristics. Most of these are very detailed skeletal features that paleontologists have described, such as a "fourth trochanter asymmetrical, with distal, lower, margin forming a steeper angle to the shaft."

Seriously? That's way too complicated.

One important thing that distinguishes dinosaurs from other reptiles is the way their legs attached to their bodies and how they stood. Dinosaurs had an **erect stance.** That means that their legs were directly underneath their bodies, as opposed to sprawling out to the side, like in other reptiles. Mammals have an erect stance as well—including you and me! But the way dinosaur leg bones fit into their hip bones, and the way they achieved their upright stance, was very different than in mammals.

The sprawling stance of an iguana is very different from the erect stance of dinosaurs and mammals (as seen in this horse).

Because we use these physical characteristics to define a dinosaur, it means we also know what *isn't* a dinosaur. Many animals that lived at the same time as the dinosaurs aren't dinosaurs because they don't have their defining physical characteristics.

Pterosaurs, the flying reptiles like *Quetzalcoatlus* and *Pteranodon*, are often called "flying dinosaurs," but they aren't. They're a separate line of reptiles that evolved independently from dinosaurs. Mosasaurs, plesiosaurs, and ichthyosaurs—the **marine reptiles** that swam in the oceans during the Mesozoic Period—weren't dinosaurs either. They evolved from a different line of reptiles long before dinosaurs arrived on the scene.

All these animals lived during the Mesozoic Period, but they weren't dinosaurs: The pterosaurs, *Pteranodon* and *Quetzalcoatlus*; the champsosaur, *Champsosaurus*; the mosasaur, *Mosasaurus*; the ichthyosaur, *Caypullisaurus*; and the plesiosaur, *Albertonectes*.

BIRDS

We now know that birds evolved from a specific group of dinosaurs. *Archaeopteryx*, from the late Jurassic Period in modern-day Germany, is often called the first bird. When *Archaeopteryx* was discovered, scientists had seen nothing like it because its fossilized remains included imprints of feathers. But it also had a long, bony tail, which living birds don't have, and instead of a beak it had jaws filled with teeth. It is a great example of a **transitional fossil,** where it shows a mix of characteristics—in this case, both dinosaur and bird.

In the 170 years since *Archaeopteryx* was discovered, we've found lots of little birdlike dinosaurs, and beginning in the 1990s, paleontologists began to find many of them with feather impressions. All of these have come from a group of dinosaurs called **coelurosaurs** *(see-LOO-roe-sawrs),* the group of dinosaurs that includes *T-rex*, the ostrich dinosaurs, and many others. Today, we

The Jurassic dinosaur *Archaeopteryx*

Nonavian dinosaurs

no longer think of *Archaeopteryx* as the first bird but as just one of many small, feathered dinosaurs.

We now know that birds are a type of dinosaur. This means that not all the dinosaurs went extinct at the end of the Cretaceous Period. One line of dinosaurs survived and is still living with us today!

Still, our fascination is with the dinosaurs that did go extinct at the end of the Cretaceous, the giants like *Tyrannosaurus* and *Apatosaurus*. To help distinguish between those dinosaurs and the ones that are still alive today (birds!), we refer to the dinosaurs that aren't birds as **nonavian dinosaurs.** And those are the ones we'll focus on.

The History of Life on Earth

We measure time in minutes, hours, days, weeks, months, and years. As we get older, decades. But as soon as we try to consider the passage of longer periods of time (centuries, or tens and hundreds of millions of years), we have difficulty understanding the concept. To help make sense of it, we use a scale that divides Earth's history into sections.

Scientists believe the Earth formed about 4.5 billion years ago, and that the earliest forms of life appeared between 4.1 and 3.8 billion years ago. This was simple, single-celled life like bacteria. The first multicellular life appeared between 2 and 2.5 billion years ago. Fungi may be the oldest multicelled life-form, and it first appeared on land around 1.3 billion years ago. Simple plants, like algae, may have evolved 1 billion years ago, and we think animal life began to evolve around 750 million years ago.

MASS EXTINCTIONS

Extinction is when an entire species ceases to exist. It is a normal part of life on Earth. Plant and animal species regularly fade out of existence because of natural processes that impact their habitat, their food supply, or their ability to reproduce. **Mass extinctions** are events that cause a big percentage of life on Earth to die out because of a cataclysmic event or a series of events. You're probably familiar with the asteroid scenario that wiped out the dinosaurs at the end of the Cretaceous Period, but science has identified five times in Earth's history when all life was nearly wiped out.

Even though these events are destructive, mass extinction events are important to life. Throughout Earth's history, mass extinction events have hit the reset button on life, allowing what had been minor species to take over in ecosystems when their dominant life-forms died out. A perfect example of this is when the nonavian dinosaurs died out at the end of the Cretaceous Period and mammals took over.

Over the next few pages, we'll discuss some of the major time periods in the history of dinosaurs, as well as how mass extinction events shaped their world.

THE MESOZOIC PERIOD
251–66 MILLION YEARS AGO

The beginning of the Mesozoic was a time of recovery after a previous extinction event, known as the Great Dying. **Dicynodonts,** like little *Lystrosaurus*, made it through and were one of the common early Triassic vertebrates. Eventually, the **rauisuchians** (large, bipedal reptiles unrelated to dinosaurs) would become the dominant predators of the Triassic. Crocodilians, dinosaurs, birds, mammals, pterosaurs, and marine reptiles like the plesiosaurs and ichthyosaurs would all evolve in the Mesozoic Period. In the Cretaceous Period, **angiosperms** (flowering plants, including trees with leaves and grasses) would evolve and, by the end of the era, come to dominate the landscape. The end-Cretaceous asteroid collision would drive the extinction of the marine reptiles, the nonavian dinosaurs, and the pterosaurs.

Lystrosaurus was one of the few large animals to make it through the Permian mass extinction.

The early Cretaceous Eumeralla Formation of Australia, featuring *Muttaburrasaurus, Diluvicursor, Leaellynasaura, Atlascopcosaurus,* unnamed ornithischian dinosaur, megaraptor, and ankylosaur

TRIASSIC MASS EXTINCTION

The extinction event that marks the end of the Triassic Period wiped out the rauisuchians (crocodile-like reptiles), the temnospondyls, and the mammal-like reptiles 201 million years ago. The dinosaurs, which appeared near the end of the Triassic Period, survived.

END-CRETACEOUS MASS EXTINCTION

About 66.5 million years ago, an asteroid that was 6 miles in diameter slammed into Earth; this impact, coupled with massive volcanic eruptions in India, wiped out the nonavian dinosaurs, the pterosaurs, the giant marine reptiles, and many other large forms of life. Mammals survived, as did birds, and both groups flourished.

THE CENOZOIC PERIOD
66 MILLION YEARS AGO TO PRESENT

The Cenozoic Period is the current period of Earth's geologic history. Dinosaurs would survive in the form of birds; however, they would never reach the dominance they held in the Mesozoic Period. Angiosperm plants would expand. Grasslands became common, providing lush feeding grounds for herds of animals. Commonly referred to as the **Age of Mammals,** the Cenozoic Period would see mammals take over and flourish in niches previously filled by nonavian dinosaurs. They would become bigger and would come to include the largest animals to populate the Earth (whales). About 2 million years ago, a small mammal in Africa would develop an erect stance and its brain would enlarge and grow more complex. It would develop language, culture, and, eventually, civilization. This one species—humans—would come to dominate the world unlike any other creature before it.

Late Pleistocene stage of the Cenozoic in North America: *Homotherium, Canis (Aenocyon) dirus* (dire wolf pack), *Camelops, Tetrameryx, Bison antiquus, Teratornis, Glyptotherium, Harringtonhippus, Arctodus, Panthera atrox* (American Lion), *Mammuthus primigenius* (woolly mammoth), *Mylohyus, Eremotherium* (juvenile), and *Odocoileus virginianus* (white-tailed deer)

Life in the Mesozoic

The Mesozoic Era, also called the "Age of Reptiles" is the time when dinosaurs lived. It began 252 million years ago and ended 66 million years ago with the mass extinction at the end of the Cretaceous. The Mesozoic is separated into three periods: the Triassic, the Jurassic, and the Cretaceous. Within each period, there are shorter stages that identify specific time periods in Earth's history.

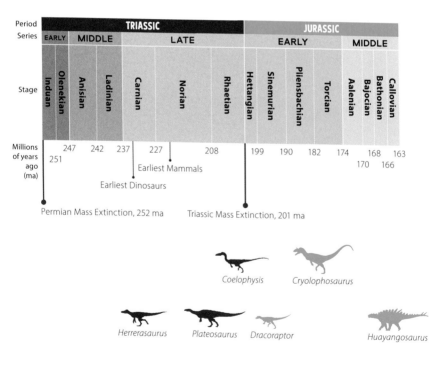

Period	TRIASSIC			JURASSIC	
Series	EARLY	MIDDLE	LATE	EARLY	MIDDLE
Stage	Induan / Olenekian	Anisian / Ladinian	Carnian / Norian / Rhaetian	Hettangian / Sinemurian / Pliensbachian / Torcian	Aalenian / Bajocian / Bathonian / Callovian

Millions of years ago (ma): 251, 247, 242, 237, 227, 208, 199, 190, 182, 174, 170, 168, 166, 163

Earliest Mammals

Earliest Dinosaurs

Permian Mass Extinction, 252 ma

Triassic Mass Extinction, 201 ma

Coelophysis

Cryolophosaurus

Herrerasaurus

Plateosaurus

Dracoraptor

Huayangosaurus

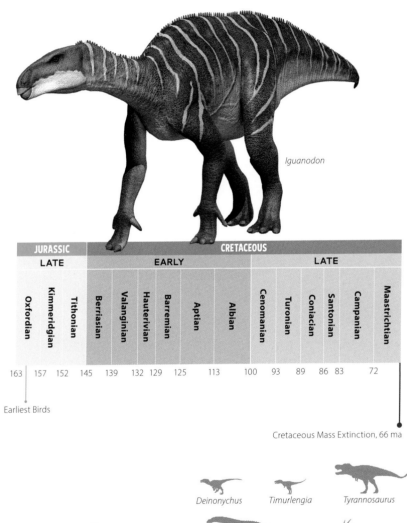

Iguanodon

JURASSIC	CRETACEOUS												
LATE	EARLY							LATE					
Oxfordian	Kimmeridgian	Tithonian	Berriasian	Valanginian	Hauterivian	Barremian	Aptian	Albian	Cenomanian	Turonian	Coniacian	Santonian	Campanian	Maastrichtian

163 | 157 | 152 | 145 | 139 | 132 | 129 | 125 | 113 | 100 | 93 | 89 | 86 | 83 | 72

Earliest Birds

Cretaceous Mass Extinction, 66 ma

Deinonychus   Timurlengia   Tyrannosaurus

Brontosaurus   Iguanodon   Argentinosaurus   Styracosaurus

THE TRIASSIC

Throughout the Triassic, all of Earth's continents were grouped together into one massive "supercontinent" called **Pangea.**

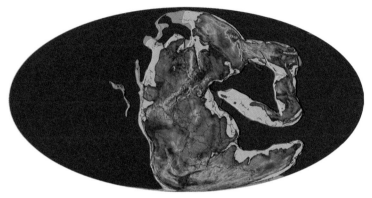

Map of the world showing the location of the continents at the start of the Triassic

The supercontinent was so massive, very little rainfall made it to the center, so most of it was hot and dry. Most life existed along the coastlines.

During the Triassic, reptiles made extraordinary advances and evolved into several major life-forms. Dinosaurs, pterosaurs, and crocodilians all evolved in the Triassic. But the dominant predators were rauisuchians, large bipedal reptiles that looked a bit like walking crocodiles. The herbivores included the dicynodonts like *Lystrosaurus*, and later the armored aetosaurs.

At first glance, plants in the Triassic would have looked very familiar. There were ferns and pine trees. Mosses and lichens clung to rocks. Cycads, which are still around today in tropical areas, and tall tree ferns would have filled out the understory of plants. Horsetails were common in marshes and along shorelines.

But if you looked across the landscape, you'd notice that some things were missing. There was no grass. Leafy shrubs and trees couldn't be found. There were no palm trees or cacti, and no flowers anywhere. All these types of plants belong to a group of plants called **angiosperms,** and they had not yet evolved, and wouldn't for another 50–60 million years.

Triassic Landscape

By the end of the Triassic Period, dinosaurs had evolved, but they were small, unimportant parts of the environment. Then, the Earth experienced another mass extinction. A huge line of volcanoes erupted in the center of the supercontinent. It was one of the largest volcanic events of all time and lasted for around 600,000 years. The result was a tremendous outpouring of ash and toxic gases that polluted the atmosphere and the oceans and blocked out the sun.

The End-Triassic extinction killed off the rauisuchians and aetosaurs, and in the following Jurassic Period, dinosaurs quickly adapted to become the dominant land vertebrates.

THE JURASSIC

During the Jurassic Period, Pangea began to break apart. Sea water flooded into the gaps between the newly formed continents, isolating them and their inhabitants from one another and setting the stage for greater adaptation, diversification, and evolution of dinosaur species. With the rauisuchians out of the picture, carnivorous dinosaurs grew bigger and became the dominant predators on land.

Plants were barely changed from the Triassic. Conifers continued to be the most common trees, and cycads, horsetails, ferns, and tree ferns were everywhere. The breakup of Pangea created pockets of wetter environments, allowing plants to colonize farther inland and create new ecosystems for the dinosaurs. Fossils of angiosperms, the flowering plants, first appear in late-Jurassic rocks, but they were rare.

Dinosaurs evolved into an ever-growing range of sizes, shapes, and types. The armored dinosaurs (the thyreophorans) evolved in the Jurassic and gave rise to stegosaurs and ankylosaurs. Sauropods grew enormous, with some reaching more than 100 feet in length.

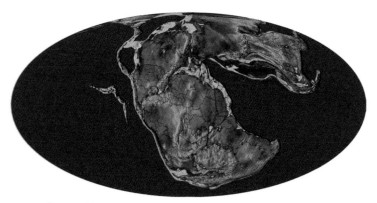

Map of the world showing the position of the continents at the start of the Jurassic

THE CRETACEOUS

During the Cretaceous Period, the continents moved near the positions we know today. The climate was warmer, and sea levels were higher. A massive ocean, the Western Interior Seaway, split the North American continent in two, and Europe was just a series of islands.

All of this set the stage for a major diversification of plants, and in the early Cretaceous, flowering plants colonized the landscape. These would become a major food source for dinosaurs, further driving adaptations and evolution. Animals would eat the seeds and fruits of these new plants and get covered in the plant's pollen. The animals moved about, sometimes great distances, and in the process, dispersed both the pollen, which falls or is blown off their skin,

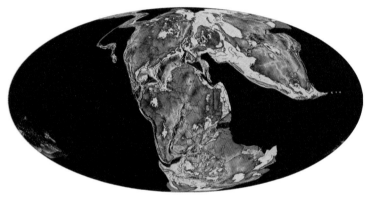

Map of the world showing the position of the continents at the start of the Cretaceous

and the seeds, which are deposited in the animals' droppings. The plants take root and adapt to take advantage of their new environment. The animals then evolve to take advantage of these new food resources, possibly developing specialized mouths and beaks, and perhaps gaining other physical advantages. Animals eat the newly evolved plants' seeds and fruits, and the cycle continues.

By the late Cretaceous, angiosperms were the dominant plant life. Flowers would have dotted the landscape, and palms would have been present.

By the end of the Cretaceous, the landscape would have looked very much as today.

Around 66 million years ago, Earth suffered a major catastrophe. An asteroid or comet 6 miles across slammed into the Gulf of Mexico at a site known now as **Chicxulub.** This impact happened at the same time that massive volcanic eruptions were occurring in India, resulting in a chain reaction of natural disasters that included tsunamis, continent-wide wildfires, ash fallout, toxic gas emissions, and global cooling that led to the extinction of the nonavian dinosaurs.

As Earth recovered from that disaster, one group of small dinosaurs survived and thrived. Throughout the Cenozoic Period, birds would repopulate the Earth

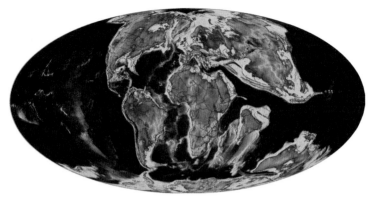

Map of the world showing the positions of the continents at the end of the Cretaceous

with over 10,000 species of dinosaurs (birds!) But they would never again match the dominance of their cousins in the Mesozoic.

An asteroid impact 66 million years ago spelled doom for the dinosaurs.

The First Dinosaurs

Dinosaurs most likely evolved from a small, bipedal reptile in the middle to late Triassic Period, around 230–235 million years ago.

The earliest dinosaurs discovered so far include *Eoraptor, Panphagia, Herrerasaurus,* and *Pisanosaurus.* These dinosaurs all date from the late Triassic Period, about 230 million years ago, and were discovered in South America.

These were all small dinosaurs that ran on two legs, with *Eoraptor* and *Pisanosaurus* measuring just 2–4 feet tall, and *Herrerasaurus* being larger at up to 17 feet long.

The early dinosaur *Herrerasaurus* chasing *Eoraptor, Pisanosaurus,* and *Panphagia* in the late Triassic.

Naming Dinosaurs

Dinosaurs are known for their long, tongue-twisting names. But how do they get those names?

Dinosaur names are split into two parts: A genus name (i.e., *Tyrannosaurus*) and a species name (*rex*). Historically, the genus name was based on Greek and Latin language and described something

The titanosaur *Futalognkosaurus*

about the dinosaur. For instance, the name *Tyrannosaurus rex* comes from the Greek *tyrannos*, meaning "tyrant," and *sauros*, meaning "lizard." The species name *rex* means "king." So, *Tyrannosaurus rex* translates to "tyrant lizard king."

Sometimes, dinosaurs are named after the location where they're found. The ankylosaur *Cedarpelta* was found in the Cedar Mountain Formation in Utah. Its name combines *Cedar* for the formation and the Greek word *pelte*, meaning "small shield" (*pelta* is a common part of ankylosaur names and refers

Far right: Dynamoterror

to the heavy armor on their back). The Australian ornithopod *Muttaburrasaurus* is named for the town Muttaburra in Queensland near where it was found, so the name means "lizard from Muttaburra."

Some dinosaur names are based on the local language from where they were discovered. The tongue-twisting name *Futalognkosaurus* (foo-tow-log-no-SAWR-us) was given to a giant sauropod from Argentina. In the local Mapudungun language, *futa* means "giant" and *lognko* means "chief," so the name translates to "giant chief lizard." The oviraptor *Citipati* is named after a Buddhist god.

Recently, paleontologists have been having a bit more fun in naming dinosaurs. The aptly named *Dynamoterror* ("powerful terror") is a newly discovered relative of *Tyrannosaurus*, and the ankylosaur *Zuul* was named after the demon god in the classic comedy *Ghostbusters*.

Zuul

Types of Dinosaurs

We group different types of dinosaurs together because they share certain physical traits. These groupings allow us to understand the relationship between different dinosaurs and build a picture of how different species evolved over time. This process is called **classification.**

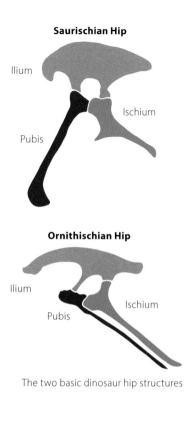

Saurischian Hip

Ilium

Ischium

Pubis

Ornithischian Hip

Ilium

Ischium

Pubis

The two basic dinosaur hip structures

At their highest level, dinosaurs are classified into two major groups based on the arrangement of their hip bones. Hips consist of three primary bones: the ilium, the ischium, and the pubis.

In **Saurischians,** the pubis points forward, whereas in **Ornithischians,** the pubis points backward.

Within the Saurischian classification, there are two major groups of dinosaurs that share this forward-pointing pubis in their hip structure: **Theropods** and **Sauropodomorphs.**

THEROPODS

Theropods are a diverse group of dinosaurs that includes some of the giant meat eaters like *Tyrannosaurus* and *Spinosaurus*, the raptor dinosaurs like *Velociraptor* and *Deinonychus*, ostrich dinosaurs like *Gallimimus*, and the small birdlike dinosaurs such as *Microraptor* and *Anchiornis*. However, they all share a few common characteristics. In addition to having a common hip structure, they all walk on two legs; that is, they are **bipedal.** They all have three toes that touch the ground. Most of the theropods were meat

Theropod dinosaurs had a range of sizes and shapes.

eaters, or carnivorous, though over time many of them adapted to become omnivores (animals that eat both meat and plants), insectivores (animals that eat insects), and even herbivores (animals that eat plants).

SAUROPODOMORPHS

Sauropodomorphs include the long-necked, long-tailed sauropod giants like *Brontosaurus* and their ancestors, the Prosauropods.

Prosauropods only lived during the late Triassic and early Jurassic. They had long necks and tails, but they were smaller than the later sauropods and walked on two legs instead of all four. Examples include *Plateosaurus* from Germany and *Massospondylus* from North America.

The Sauropods evolved in the early Jurassic and continued throughout the Mesozoic. They're also characterized by long necks and tails, but these animals were fully quadrupedal—that is, they walked on all four feet. By the middle of the Jurassic, some of them had become enormous—up to 100 feet long and the largest land animals to walk the Earth. All the sauropodomorphs that have been discovered are herbivores.

Sauropodomorph dinosaurs

ORNITHISCHIANS

Ornithischians are known from the late Triassic at the very base of the dinosaur family tree. They started out as small, bipedal plant eaters just a few feet long, and many kept that body plan and lifestyle all the way to the extinction of the nonavian dinosaurs.

Ornithischian dinosaurs

Other ornithischians evolved into a range of animals with varied lifestyles, including the armored *Stegosaurus* and *Ankylosaurus*, the horned *Triceratops*, and the duckbilled dinosaurs with elaborate head crests.

How Dinosaurs Lived

DIET

We tend not to think about our teeth much unless we lose one or are at the dentist. But teeth are one of the most important parts of our bodies; by examining an animal's teeth, we can learn a lot about the creature.

If you look at your teeth in a mirror, one of the first things you'll notice is that they have several different shapes. In the front, you have incisors that are useful for nipping and cutting both plants and meat. Next, you have canine teeth, the longer pointed ones that are for tearing food. Lastly, you have molars that are used for chewing and grinding. This arrangement of having different types of teeth that serve different purposes is typical in mammals. But dinosaur teeth were different. Most dinosaurs only had one type of tooth in their mouth.

In meat-eating dinosaurs, their teeth were typically long, curved, and knife-like. If you look very closely, you'll see that the front and back edges of their teeth have tiny bumps on them called **serrations** that make them look like a saw blade or a steak knife. And just like with a saw or knife, those serrations helped them slice through the thick skin and meat of their prey. So, if we find a dinosaur that has long, curved teeth with serrated edges, we know that it was a meat eater.

This is the tooth of the meat-eating dinosaur *Carcharodontosaurus*. Note the serrations on the edge.

The teeth of spinosaurs are a bit different. They're long and sharp, but instead of being flattened and knife-like, they're round, more like a spike, and don't have serrated edges. Teeth like these are very useful for catching and holding on to slippery prey like fish.

A *Spinosaurus* tooth

The teeth of plant-eating dinosaurs were very different. The small ornithischians, ankylosaurs, and stegosaurs had teeth that were small and leaf- or diamond-shaped. They also had serrated edges, which helped them to slice through plants and leaves. Instead of molars to grind up their food, some dinosaurs, like the horned ceratopsians and the duckbilled hadrosaurs, developed multiple rows of hundreds of teeth that acted as grinding surfaces called **dental batteries.**

Many plant-eating dinosaurs also had sharp beaks that helped them slice through plants and twigs.

Sauropod teeth came in a variety of shapes and sizes. Some were like bigger versions of the ornithischian teeth, but others were pencil- or peg-like and would have been used to strip vegetation off the branches of trees.

REPRODUCTION & PARENTAL CARE

Like all living reptiles, dinosaurs reproduced by laying eggs. We know this because many dinosaur eggs have been found from several different dinosaurs, including oviraptors, titanosaurs, hadrosaurs, therizinosaurs, troodontids, prosauropods, and ceratopsians. Sometimes we even find the fossilized remains of embryos inside the eggs, which provide us with a unique understanding of how the dinosaur developed.

All dinosaurs appear to have laid their eggs in nests, again just like modern birds and reptiles do; however, all dinosaur nests were on the ground rather than up in trees. Many of the nests appear to have been dug into the ground, and then covered with plant material to camouflage and protect the nest after the eggs were laid. Many dinosaurs had large nesting grounds that were used by either a great number of individuals or, in some cases, herds or colonies. Huge grounds of titanosaur nests have been found in South America. At a site known as Egg Mountain in Montana, a colony of *Maiasaura* (a type of duckbilled dinosaur) nests have been discovered.

Exactly what happened to the eggs after they were laid seems to have varied depending on the type of dinosaur. In the case of the titanosaur nests, the parents appear to have abandoned the nests and left the eggs to incubate. Once hatched, the baby titanosaurs were left on their own to survive. The nests of the prosauropod *Massospondylus* and the *Maiasaura* nesting ground at Egg Mountain show evidence that the eggs were tended to by the parents and that the baby dinosaurs were cared for after hatching.

An adult *Maiasaura* tending to her hatchlings

SOCIAL BEHAVIOR—HERDING, MIGRATION, AND PACK BEHAVIOR

Many types of dinosaurs show evidence of gathering in groups. Evidence of this behavior exists in the form of **mass death assemblages or bone beds,** which are fossil accumulations of multiple individuals—sometimes thousands of them, sometimes just a few—that all died at or near the same time, and at the same place.

It's unclear from the fossil record what brought all these animals together and how they all died, but bone beds have been found for both plant-eating and carnivorous dinosaurs. The ceratopsian dinosaurs *Pachyrhinosaurus* and *Centrosaurus* are both known from massive bone beds that have both young and old individuals, showing they probably lived and migrated in herds.

Herds of dinosaurs roam through what is now Dinosaur Provincial Park in Alberta, Canada.

Bone beds of meat-eating dinosaurs have been found, as well, but usually contain fewer individuals. The enormous meat-eater *Mapusaurus* is known from a bone bed containing six individuals of various ages. A 10-ton block of rock was discovered in Utah that contains the skeletons of at least a dozen *Utahraptors* ranging in size from juveniles just 3 feet long to adults up to 15 feet. And in New Mexico, hundreds of *Coelophysis* have been found at a site known as Ghost Ranch. Exactly what led to the death of all these predators at one place and time is unclear. They may represent family groups or pack behavior. We just can't be sure, and any speculation is just that: best guesses based on the information available.

SOUND AND VOCALIZATIONS

Did dinosaurs make sounds? Most animals today vocalize in some way—lions roar, birds tweet and sing, pigs grunt. Even crocodiles bellow and hiss. Some animals communicate by stomping the ground or making splashes in water.

Swarms of *Allosaurus* attack a mired *Diplodocus*.

We'll probably never know for sure whether dinosaurs made sounds, but given that many were social animals living in herds and their close relationship to birds, they probably did.

Some scientists have done a lot of work to determine whether dinosaurs made noises, and if so, what type. They've discovered that it's highly unlikely that *Tyrannosaurus* could roar, as is shown in some movies. More likely, it made some sort of low-pitched grunting or rumbling sound. Some of the smaller dinosaurs, like *Velociraptor* and *Archaeopteryx,* may have chirped or screeched like modern birds. Some scientists think hadrosaurs like *Parasaurolophus* may have used their large crests as resonating chambers to produce calls.

Parasaurolophus may have used its crest to make vocalizations.

As fun as it is to imagine what an ancient world full of bellowing and chirping dinosaurs might have sounded like, we'll probably never really know if that was the case. The soft tissues needed to make noises don't fossilize—and even if they did, we wouldn't be able to recreate the sound accurately.

Tyrannosaurus "chirped" to attract mates.

DINOSAUR INJURIES

Another clue to the social behavior of dinosaurs is the evidence we've found of wounds found in dinosaur bones. These wounds could have been caused by injuries or illnesses and are called **pathologies.** We can study these pathologies and determine a lot about how the animal lived based on their nature and cause.

The Science Museum of Minnesota displays a *Triceratops* skeleton, and just above the eye on one side of the skull is a hole that is not part of the regular anatomy. It appears to have been made by the impact of a large, sharp object. By measuring the hole, scientists have determined that it was most likely made by the horn of another *Triceratops* and think that it happened when the two animals rammed into one another, either in a territorial battle or a battle for mates!

Adult *Triceratops* battle

We've also found deep scars on the skulls of several large carnivorous dinosaurs that match perfectly with the teeth of that species, suggesting that these large predators chomped and bit down on each other in battles.

Two *Albertosaurus* fight for dominance.

An *Edmontosaurus* skeleton has been found with a chunk taken out of its tail—and the chunk matched perfectly with the bite of *Tyrannosaurus rex*! But even more amazing is that the bones appear to have healed, meaning that the duckbill survived the attack!

A *Tyrannosaurus* chomps down on *Edmontosaurus's* tail.

We've even found bone pathologies that show that dinosaurs got cancer, in addition to healed leg fractures showing that a dinosaur survived an injury and lived out its life with a limp.

We normally think that fossils just show us what a dinosaur might have looked like. But by studying the details of those fossils, what kind of environment they came from, and what evidence they show, we can learn a lot about but how that dinosaur lived.

SCALES

One thing you'll notice about all the reconstructions of *Iguanodon* is that it's shown covered in scales. Dinosaurs are typically depicted covered in scales, but were they? When they were first discovered, dinosaurs' close relation to reptiles suggested they were similar in appearance, and so the assumption was that their bodies were scaly.

Over the years, we've found patches of dinosaur skin that have been preserved in the fossil record. We've found examples of horned dinosaurs (*Centrosaurus, Triceratops, Psittacosaurus*), duckbills (*Edmontosaurus, Corythosaurus, Brachylophosaurus, Hypacrosaurus*), large meat eaters (*Tyrannosaurus, Carnotaurus, Daspletosaurus*), ankylosaurs (*Borealopelta*), and stegosaurs (*Stegosaurus*), just to name a few. And in all of these cases, they show that the dinosaurs were covered in scales. There are a lot of

The nodosaur *Borealopelta*

different sizes and shapes
of scales found in these skin
impressions, but they were
all non-overlapping (unlike a
snake, which has scales that
overlap each other) and are
usually round or hexagonal
(six-sided) in shape. Even the

All dinosaurs had scales covering at
least part of their body.

feathered dinosaurs that we've found, like *Archaeopteryx* and *Caudipteryx*, have scales on their feet and
on their faces.

ARMOR

Many of the plant-eating dinosaurs are known for
their elaborate armor. The tall plates of *Stegosaurus* and the horns and frill on *Triceratops* are unlike
anything seen in the animal kingdom today. The tank

dinosaurs, like *Ankylosaurus,* evolved huge tail clubs, and many had huge plates and spikes that stuck out from their shoulders and sides.

Ever since the first armored dinosaurs were found, it was assumed that all these spikes and horns and plates were defensive weapons evolved to protect the plant eater from predators. But was that really the case?

The heavily plated back of *Ankylosaurus* certainly would have given it some protection against *Tyrannosaurus*. But the elaborate horns of *Triceratops* may have served as a signaling device to attract females or warn off rivals. The plates of the *Stegosaurus* were thin and probably offered little protection, though they might have been brightly colored and attracted other stegosaurs. The long spikes on its tail, called the **thagomizer,** were clearly used as a weapon, and we've found evidence of damage done to an *Allosaurus* that appears to have been hit by them.

So, which is it: defense or display?

If we look at living herbivores, we can get some clues. There aren't any living animals that have horns, spikes, and plates like dinosaurs. There are some species of deer and antelope that have impressive antlers, such as moose and elk. In these cases, as the animal matures, the antlers are used as displays to attract mates, but, if attacked by a predator, the creature

Dinosaur armor and display: The stegosaur *Stegosaurus*; the ankylosaurs *Cedarpelta*, *Jakapil*, *Stegouros*, and *Gastonia*; the horned dinosaurs *Triceratops* and *Styracosaurus*; and the primitive thyreophoran *Scutellosaurus*

can also use those features to defend itself. This was probably the case with dinosaurs as well. They likely used their armor to either attract mates or intimidate rivals or predators, but, if needed, they could also use them to defend themselves.

LIPS

Lips? On dinosaurs?

We're used to seeing predatory dinosaurs with their big teeth hanging out over their lower jaws. But new research is challenging that look.

Lips are soft tissues that cover an animal's teeth. They protect the teeth in a couple of ways. First, they keep the teeth from drying out by holding them in the saliva (liquid) that exists in the mouth. Secondly, they protect the teeth from damage and abrasion (scraping and rubbing).

We can look at living reptiles for some clues about whether dinosaurs had lips. Living predatory reptiles fall into two categories when it comes to mouths and lips. Lizards and snakes have lips. Even the largest lizard, the Komodo Dragon, has lips that cover its teeth when its mouth is closed. Crocodilians don't have lips. Their teeth stick out even when their mouths are closed.

Research has shown that the jaws and their arrangement of teeth in dinosaurs is more like the jaws and teeth of lizards than those of crocodiles. It has also

The predatory dinosaur *Teratophoneus* shown with and without lips

shown that the outward-pointing nature of crocodile teeth is probably something that evolved as they became semiaquatic and were able to keep their teeth moist and protected while in water. Ancient, extinct crocodiles were not aquatic, and their teeth and jaws were more like those of dinosaurs and lizards.

It makes sense, then, that predatory dinosaurs had the same kind of lips we see in other animals, to keep their teeth moist and protected.

A brightly colored *Regaliceratops* and *Albertosaurus* battle in the late Cretaceous.

COLORING

What color were dinosaurs? Historically, they've been portrayed as kind of drab gray, brown, or green. More recently, researchers and paleoartists (artists who attempt to depict prehistoric life through scientific evidence) have gotten bold, showing dinosaurs with flamboyant colors and dramatic patterns. Much of this is based on the coloration of living animals. Both predator and prey species display elaborate patterns to camouflage themselves—animals like tigers, giraffes, and zebras are all boldly colored. And many reptile species have bright coloring over part or most of their bodies to help attract mates or scare off would-be enemies. Many of these examples influence how dinosaurs are depicted.

But do we really know what color dinosaurs were? In some cases, the answer is yes! Scientists have discovered that when the fossil preservation is extremely good, certain cells can be fossilized and examined under the microscope. The cells, called **melanosomes,** determine pigment or color. Scientists can "read" these cells and, by comparing them to the same type of cells in living animals, determine what the color the fossilized animal was. This is a very rare occurrence. A well-preserved fossil of the primitive horned dinosaur *Psittacosaurus* has revealed that it was dark reddish brown on its side and back, with larger black scales on its shoulder. Its belly was lighter, and its face was black and mottled reddish brown and white. A fossil of *Sinosauropteryx*, a small, feathered meat eater from China, was light brown with a white underside, and its tail was striped brown and white. And the exquisitely preserved fossil of *Borealopelta* showed us it was also dark reddish brown on top with a lighter underside (this pattern, with a darker top and lighter underneath, is called **countershading,** and we see it a lot in nature).

FEATHERS

We now know that some dinosaurs were feathered. The fact that birds are dinosaurs proves this, but even some of the nonavian dinosaurs were feathered. All the feathered nonavian dinosaurs that have been discovered so far are theropods. The largest feathered dinosaur we know of was the *Yutyrannus* from early-Cretaceous China, measuring around 20 feet long. The feathered dinosaurs didn't have the same type of feathers covering their bodies as modern birds. They had **protofeathers,** which were simple coverings that would have resembled fur. However, several dinosaurs do show evidence of having longer, more birdlike wing feathers.

Feathered *Sinosauropteryx*

The feathered tyrannosaur *Yutyrannus* inspects its nest.

Other groups of dinosaurs have been found with coverings that may or may not have been protofeathers. *Psittacosaurus*

Kulindadromeus may have been covered in feathers or some other type of soft tissue fiber.

had a line of long quills running along the top of its tail. Similar structures are seen in the ornithischian *Tianyulong*. Another ornithischian, *Kulindadromeus* from the middle Jurassic in Russia, had a covering similar to protofeathers and longer, more ornate structures on its shoulders and legs. In all these

A juvenile *T-rex* with feathers

cases, paleontologists are divided on whether these structures are protofeathers or some other type of structure altogether.

The big question people ask is, "Was the *T-rex* feathered?" The simple answer is we don't know. Skin samples have been found for *Tyrannosaurus*, but none of them show feather impressions. Just scales. Some researchers believe it may have been feathered as a juvenile, and then lost its feathers as it got older. Hopefully, new discoveries in the future will shed some light on the issue and give us answers.

Where Dinosaur Fossils are Found

Dinosaur remains are found on every major continent and land mass, including Antarctica (which was much farther north in the Mesozoic), Madagascar, Greenland, and Australia. But regardless of which continent they're on, the locations where dinosaur fossils are found share a few things in common:

Mesozoic-aged rocks are on the surface and easy to access.

In order to find fossils of dinosaurs, we have to look for them in rocks from the time when dinosaurs lived. There are very few places on Earth where rocks from the Mesozoic Period are right on the surface. In the 66 million years since the end of the Cretaceous, erosion has buried most Mesozoic rocks under sediment that can be hundreds of feet deep. In a few

Fauna of the Hell Creek Formation: *Edmontosaurus, Pachycephalosaurus, Quetzal-coatlus, Tyrannosaurus, Dakotaraptor, Deinosuchus, Ankylosaurus, Thescelosaurus, Ornithomimus, Triceratops, Edmontonia*

places, however, geologic processes have pushed the Mesozoic rocks to the surface or have eroded the sediment to expose them.

They are found in sedimentary rock layers.

There are many different types of rock formations on Earth, and only a few kinds preserve dinosaur fossils. For dinosaur remains to have fossilized, the animal must have died in a location where the body was quickly covered up by sediment, primarily sand or mud. These environments typically exist in floodplains, where flowing water deposits layers of mud and sand, and in deserts, where dry sand can quickly be blown and bury a body. One of the sad facts of paleontology

is that there are likely thousands of types of dinosaurs that we'll never know about because they lived in environments that did not favor fossilization. Environments like highland regions that are typically rocky, or vast plains that saw localized rain but little transfer of sediments to bury bodies.

Around the world, there are some dinosaur "hot spots," locations that were particularly favorable to the preservation and fossilization of dinosaur remains for long periods of time. These locations, where ancient rock layers are exposed on the surface, are called "formations."

Throughout this book, you'll see the abbreviation "ma" which stands for *millions of years ago*.

Although they're often confused with dinosaurs, these ancient reptiles are evolutionarily closer to mammals than they are to dinosaurs.

DIMETRODON

Pronunciation: dye-MEH-trow-dawn

Meaning: Two measures of teeth

Lifestyle: Carnivore

Location: North America (New Mexico, Texas, Oklahoma); Europe (Germany)

Time Period: Permian (Cisuralian) 295–272 ma

Size: 15 ft

Dimetrodon is familiar to many people because of the tall sail on its back. Its sail may have been used to help control its body temperature by absorbing heat from the sun, or it may have been a display structure to help attract mates and threaten rivals.

INOSTRANCEVIA

Pronunciation: inn-ah-stran-SIH-vee-ah

Meaning: After Russian geologist Aleksandr Inostrantsev

Lifestyle: Carnivore

Location: Europe (Russia)

Time Period: Permian (Lopingian) 259–252 ma

Size: 9.8 ft

Inostrancevia belonged to a group of saber-toothed synapsids called **gorgonopsids.** These predators featured long, sharp canine teeth and were the apex predators of their ecosystems. Their remains have been found in Russia, South Africa, Niger, and China. While most gorgonopsids were around 3–5 feet long, *Inostrancevia* grew huge and would have been a formidable predator.

The first true dinosaurs are known from the late Triassic in rock formations in South America.

EORAPTOR

Pronunciation: ee-oh-RAP-tore

Meaning: Dawn thief

Lifestyle: Carnivore

Location: South America (Argentina)

Time Period: Late Triassic (Carnian) 231–228 ma

Size: 5.5 ft

While it looks like a small theropod, the first dinosaurs had internal features that make them difficult to classify. Their bones seem to have characteristics of all the major groups of dinosaurs (which is expected of an animal at the base of the evolutionary tree). Since its discovery, *Eoraptor* has been classified as a theropod, an ornithischian, and, currently, a **sauropodmorph,** the term used to describe primitive sauropods.

HERRERASAURUS

Pronunciation: her-RAIR-oh-SAWR-us

Meaning: Herrerra's lizard

Lifestyle: Carnivore

Location: South America (Argentina)

Time Period: Late Triassic (Carnian) 231–228 ma

Size: 20 ft

Although primitive, *Herrerasaurus* is clearly a predator and is currently classified as a theropod. It was one of the very first large-bodied dinosaurian predators to have evolved, and similar theropods *(Chindesaurus)* existed in North America around the same time.

PISANOSAURUS

Pronunciation: pih-san-oh-SAWR-us

Meaning: Pisano's lizard

Lifestyle: Herbivore

Location: South America (Argentina)

Time Period: Late Triassic (Carnian) 229 ma

Size: 3 ft

Pisanosaurus is the earliest ornithischian that has been discovered. It was a very small animal, just 3 feet in length. Like all these early dinosaurs, many scientists still debate whether *Pisanosaurus* is really an ornithischian, or if it is even a dinosaur. In addition to these early dinosaurs, paleontologists have found fossils of rauisuchians and other large carnivores that may have preyed on *Pisanosaurus* in the same area.

PANPHAGIA

Pronunciation: pan-fah-GEE-ah

Meaning: Eat all

Lifestyle: Omnivore

Location: South America (Argentina)

Time Period: Late Triassic (Carnian) 231 ma

Size: 4.5 ft

Panphagia is another small dinosaur and appears to be the earliest known sauropod—the group of dinosaurs that would evolve into *Brontosaurus* and *Argentinosaurus*, which are the largest land animals to have ever lived. *Panphagia's* teeth show that it was transitioning from being a meat eater to an herbivore, with the front teeth being sharp and bladelike, and its back teeth being more leaf-shaped like a typical herbivore.

COELOPHYSIS

Pronunciation: see-loe-FYE-sis

Meaning: Hollow form

Lifestyle: Carnivore

Location: North America (New Mexico, Arizona)

Time Period: Late Triassic (Carnian to Rhaetian) 228–200 ma

Size: 9 ft

Coelophysis is one of the best-known early dinosaurs, thanks to the discovery of over 1,000 specimens in the Ghost Ranch site of New Mexico. The accumulation of so many animals that died at the same time has led to speculation that *Coelophysis* congregated in herds or flocks.

LILIENSTERNUS

Pronunciation: lih-lee-in-STERN-us

Meaning: Of Count Lilienstern

Lifestyle: Carnivore

Location: Europe (Germany, Switzerland)

Time Period: Late Triassic (Norian) 228–201 ma

Size: 17 ft

Liliensternus was a large predator that likely preyed upon *Plateosaurus*, which lived in the same environment. It would have been a swift, nimble predator. We only have fragmentary remains of *Liliensternus*, so much of its appearance is based on other similar dinosaurs such as *Coelophysis* and *Dilophosaurus*.

CRYOLOPHOSAURUS

Pronunciation: kry-oh-low-foe-SAWR-us

Meaning: Frozen crested lizard

Lifestyle: Carnivore

Location: Antarctica

Time Period: Early Jurassic (Pliensbachian) 186–182 ma

Size: 21 ft

During the Mesozoic era, the world was much warmer and temperate. Conditions in Antarctica were subtropical and capable of supporting large animals like *Cryolophosaurus*. The Hanson Formation, where *Cryolophosaurus* was found, has also yielded the remains of pterosaurs, small ornithischians, prosauropods (including *Glacialisaurus*), and other smaller theropods.

DILOPHOSAURUS

Pronunciation: dye-LOH-fuh-SAWR-us

Meaning: Two-crested lizard

Lifestyle: Carnivore

Location: North America (Arizona)

Time Period: Early Jurassic (Sinemurian) 193 ma

Size: 23 ft

Unlike its appearance in popular movies, *Dilophosaurus* did not have a neck frill, and there's no evidence that it spit venom (though it may have!). Also, *Dilophosaurus* grew much larger than depicted. Along with *Cryolophosaurus*, it was one of the earliest large-bodied predators that has been discovered so far.

MONOLOPHOSAURUS

Pronunciation:
mah-noh-loff-oh-SAWR-us

Meaning: Single-crested lizard

Lifestyle: Carnivore

Location: Asia (China)

Time Period: Middle Jurassic (Bathonian to Callovian) 168–163 ma

Size: 18 ft

China has informed our knowledge of many middle Jurassic predators. Most are known from fragmentary remains, but a nearly complete skeleton, including the skull, of *Monolophosaurus* has been found. Its most notable feature is the impressive crest running along the full length of its snout. When the creature was alive, the crest was probably brightly colored and used to attract a mate.

Despite a reputation for being huge predators, not all theropods were large. Many were relatively small and fed on mammals and insects.

ARCHAEOPTERYX

Pronunciation: ar-kee-OP-ter-ix

Meaning: Ancient wing

Lifestyle: Carnivore

Location: Europe (Germany)

Time Period: Late Jurassic (Tithonian) 150–145 ma

Size: 20 in

Archaeopteryx was originally believed to be the "first bird." We now recognize *Archaeopteryx* to be a type of raptor dinosaur. Analysis of the feather impressions has revealed that at least some of its feathers were dark—probably black. We're still unsure if *Archaeopteryx* was able to fly by flapping its wings (this is called "powered flight") or if it just glided among the trees.

COMPSOGNATHUS

Pronunciation: kohmp-sawg-NATH-us

Meaning: Elegant jaw

Lifestyle: Carnivore

Location: Europe (Germany, France)

Time Period: Late Jurassic (Tithonian) 150 ma

Size: 30 in

For a long time, *Compsognathus* was the smallest known dinosaur. It lived at the same time and place as *Archaeopteryx*. Many restorations show *Compsognathus* with feathers; however, there is no evidence of feathers being preserved in the known fossils.

MONONYKUS

Pronunciation: MON-oh-NYE-kus

Meaning: One claw

Lifestyle: Insectivore (?)

Location: Asia (Mongolia)

Time Period: Late Cretaceous (Maastrichtian) 70 ma

Size: 3.9 ft

Mononykus belongs to a group of dinosaurs called **Alverezasaurids.** These were small, bipedal dinosaurs who only had a single finger that sported a large, curved claw. Scientists believe they were insectivores and may have used their large claw to rip open termite mounds, though there is no direct evidence for this. All known alverezasaurids are from the Cretaceous Period.

SINOSAUROPTERYX

Pronunciation: SYE-no-sawr-OP-ter-ex

Meaning: Chinese dragon feather or Chinese lizard wing

Lifestyle: Carnivore

Location: Asia (China)

Time Period: Early Cretaceous (Barremian) 124–126 ma

Size: 27 in

Sinosauropteryx was one of the first dinosaurs whose pigmentation was determined. We now know that its feathers were brownish red and that its tail had lighter stripes. Known from the famous Yixian Formation, it would have lived alongside other feathered dinosaurs and birds. *Sinosauropteryx* was closely related to *Compsognathus*, which lived much earlier in the Jurassic Period. One specimen has been found with the remains of a lizard in its stomach region, giving an indication to its diet.

SAURORNITHOIDES

Pronunciation: sore-or-nith-OY-dees

Meaning: Lizard bird form

Lifestyle: Carnivore

Location: Asia (Mongolia)

Time Period: Late Cretaceous (Campanian) 75 ma

Size: 6 ft

Saurornithoides was a member of the troodontid group of theropods. The troodontids were small, birdlike predators that were common across Asia and North America during the Cretaceous Period. Remains of it were found in the Mongolian Djadochta Formation, which had a rich and diverse population of small mammals and lizards on which *Saurornithoides* probably fed.

CHILESAURUS

Pronunciation: chih-lee-SAWR-us

Meaning: Chile lizard

Lifestyle: Herbivore

Location: South America (Chile)

Time Period: Late Jurassic (Tithonian) 245 ma

Size: 10 ft

Chilesaurus was an unusual dinosaur. It appears to have been a theropod, which are typically meat eaters or omnivores, but it had the leaf-shaped teeth characteristic of ornithischians. It only had two fingers on its hand, like the tyrannosaurs. Some scientists believe *Chilesaurus* is ornithischian, and that the theropod-type features are an example of **convergent evolution,** a process where unrelated animals evolve similar physical characteristics because they live in similar environments.

SPINOSAURUS

Pronunciation: SPY-nuh-SAWR-us

Meaning: Spine lizard

Lifestyle: Carnivore

Location: Africa (Egypt, Morocco)

Time Period: Late Cretaceous (Cenomanian to Turonian) 99–93 ma

Size: 50 ft

Spinosaurus has become well-known since its appearance in popular films featuring dinosaurs; however, its appearance in life was quite different than how it has been depicted. *Spinosaurus* had long and heavy forearms, leading some researchers to believe it may have been quadrupedal. Its tail was tall and flattened side-to-side, which means it may have been partly aquatic in its lifestyle. *Spinosaurus* was among the largest predatory dinosaurs to have existed.

BARYONYX

Pronunciation: Bah-ree-ON-ix

Name Meaning: Heavy claw

Lifestyle: Carnivore

Location: Europe (England, Spain, Portugal)

Time Period: Early Cretaceous (Barremian) 130–125 ma

Size: 33 ft

Remains of this dinosaur were found in the Wessex Formation of England, which is one of the premier dinosaur sites in Europe. *Baryonyx* sported a huge claw on its thumb, which it may have used to catch fish. Its long jaws were filled with conical teeth; however, despite their size, its jaws were relatively weak, meaning it probably couldn't handle struggling prey. Unlike most of its spinosaur relatives, *Baryonyx* does not appear to have had a tall sail on its back.

ICHTHYOVENATOR
Pronunciation: ick-thee-oh-VEN-ah-tore

Meaning: Fish hunter

Lifestyle: Carnivore

Location: Asia (Laos)

Time Period: Early Cretaceous (Aptian) 125–113 ma

Size: 27 ft

One of the smaller spinosaurs, the presence of *Ichthyovenator* in Asia shows that the spinosaurs were a wide-ranging group, with representatives having been found in Asia, Africa, Europe, and South America. Ichthyovenator had the tall sail on its back typical of the spinosaurs, but there was a notch above the hips that split the sail into two parts. Other dinosaurs found in the area include sauropods, iguanodonts, and small ceratopsians (horned dinosaurs).

IRRITATOR
Pronunciation: EAR-ih-tay-tor

Meaning: Irritating one

Lifestyle: Carnivore

Location: South America (Brazil)

Time Period: Early Cretaceous (Albian) 113–110 ma

Size: 33 ft

Irritator is only known from a nearly complete skull and is notable in being the only spinosaur known from South America (another discovery named *Angaturama* is probably another example of *Irritator*). Like most other spinosaurs, it is assumed that *Irritator* was primarily a fish eater, based on the shape of its teeth. The Romualdo Formation in Brazil, where *Irritator* was found, is mostly known for the number of pterosaurs (flying reptiles) that have been found there.

GIGANOTOSAURUS

Pronunciation: JIH-gih-no-to-SAWR-us

Meaning: Giant southern lizard

Lifestyle: Carnivore

Location: South America (Patagonia)

Time Period: Late Cretaceous (Cenomanian) 99–95 ma

Size: 50 ft

Giganotosaurus may have been the largest carnivore to have ever walked on Earth. While it probably reached about the same length as *Spinosaurus*, it was a heavier, bulkier animal. It lived at the time when giant sauropods roamed through South America, and its size may have been an adaptation to hunt these giant beasts.

MAPUSAURUS

Pronunciation: mah-poo-SAWR-us

Meaning: Earth lizard

Lifestyle: Carnivore

Location: South America (Patagonia)

Time Period: Late Cretaceous (Turonian) 93–89 ma

Size: 40 ft

The remains of *Mapusaurus* have been found in the same rock layers and location as the giant sauropod *Argentinosaurus*, and while it probably couldn't take down a healthy adult, it likely would have preyed on juveniles. *Mapusaurus* was found in a bone bed containing up to nine individuals of varying ages. It's unclear whether this is a pack, a family group, or a predator death trap of unrelated individuals.

TYRANNOTITAN

Pronunciation: tyr-ran-oh-TYE-tahn

Meaning: Tyrant titan

Lifestyle: Carnivore

Location: South America (Patagonia)

Time Period: Early Cretaceous (Aptian) 118 ma

Size: 43 ft

Not to be confused with the famous *Tyrannosaurus rex*, *Tyrannotitan* was a carcharodontosaurid that lived 52 million years earlier. The early Cretaceous of South America seems to have been teeming with large-bodied predators, and the carcharodontosaurs were the apex predators. *Tyrannotitan* and *Acrocanthosaurus* are geologically the oldest carcharodontosaurs, having lived 15–20 million years before others that have been found.

CARCHARODONTOSAURUS

Pronunciation: kar-kar-oh-DON-tuh-SAWR-us

Meaning: Shark-toothed lizard

Lifestyle: Carnivore

Location: Africa (Egypt, Morocco)

Time Period: Late Cretaceous (Cenomanian) 99–94 ma

Size: 41 ft

Carcharodontosaurus was the first carcharodontosaur to be discovered and the group is named after it. *Carcharodontosaurus* lived at about the same time and place as *Spinosaurus*, as well as a couple of other large predators. It's unusual to find so many large predators all coexisting; however, it's believed that each one may have fed on a specific group or type of prey animal, with *Spinosaurus* being primarily a fish eater and scavenger, while *Carcharodontosaurus* may have actively preyed on other dinosaurs.

ACROCANTHOSAURUS

Pronunciation:
AK-roe-kan-thoe-SAWR-us

Meaning: High-spined lizard

Lifestyle: Carnivore

Location: North America (USA, Wyoming, Oklahoma, Texas)

Time Period: Early Cretaceous (Aptian to Albian) 113–110 ma

Size: 38 ft

Acrocanthosaurus is one of just a few carcharodontosaurs known from northern continents. This massive predator prowled the western US during the early Cretaceous. *Acrocanthosaurus* is remarkable because of its long back spines which, while not as tall as *Spinosaurus*, would have given it a sail-backed appearance. *Acrocanthosaurus'* primary prey was most likely the large-bodied ornithischian *Tenontosaurus*, whose remains are quite common.

CARNOTAURUS

Pronunciation: kahrn-uh-TAWR-us

Meaning: Meat-eating bull

Lifestyle: Carnivore

Location: South America (Brazil)

Time Period: Late Cretaceous (Maastrichtian) 71–69 ma

Size: 23 ft

Carnotaurus is known from its appearance in several popular movies. It is unique in having a pair of large horns above its eyes, giving it a bull-like appearance, and inspiring its discoverers to name it the "meat-eating bull." Though not as large as it's been depicted in movies, *Carnotaurus* had extremely long hind limbs, a feature typical of fast-running animals. Skin impressions were found when *Carnotaurus* was discovered, and they showed that it had large scutes or osteoderms running down its sides.

MAJUNGASAURUS

Pronunciation: mah-jun-gah-SAWR-us

Meaning: Majunga lizard

Lifestyle: Carnivore

Location: Africa (Madagascar)

Time Period: Late Cretaceous (Maastrichtian) 70–66 ma

Size: 23 ft

Majungasaurus was unique in having a wrinkled appearance to the bones on its snout. Like all abelisaurids, *Majungasaurus* had extremely small forelimbs that had become entirely useless. They likely preyed upon some of the smaller dinosaurs that populated Madagascar during the late Cretaceous, but they also may have fed on each other. Bones of Majungasaurus have been found that have tooth marks from another Majungasaurus—evidence of cannibalism!

RAJASAURUS

Pronunciation: RAH-jah-SAWR-us

Meaning: Princely lizard

Lifestyle: Carnivore

Location: Asia (India)

Time Period: Late Cretaceous (Maastrichtian) 67 ma

Size: 22 ft

Over the years, the number of dinosaurs known from India has been limited, but over the past couple of decades that's changed. Nearly all the abelisaurids are known from the southern continents that once made up Gondwana. At the time *Rajasaurus* lived, India was an island, having split from the main continent of Gondwana. *Rajasaurus* had a short horn on its forehead that may have been used for display or for head-butting with each other.

RUGOPS

Pronunciation: RUH-gahps

Meaning: Wrinkled face

Lifestyle: Carnivore

Location: Africa (Egypt, Morocco, Niger)

Time Period: Late Cretaceous (Cenomanian) 95 ma

Size: 17.5 ft

While most of the abelisaurids are known from South America, the remains of several species have also been found in Africa, Asia, and possibly Europe. *Rugops* represents one of the African lines of abelisaurids. Its remains were found in Niger. Its name refers to the wrinkled structure on the bones of its snout, which is typical of bone found to have been covered in keratin (horn). *Rugops* lived alongside the giant predators *Spinosaurus* and *Carcharodontosaurus*. It is believed that these predators went after different prey and did not compete with one another for food.

VELOCIRAPTOR

Pronunciation: veh-loss-ih-RAP-tor

Meaning: Fast thief

Lifestyle: Carnivore

Location: Asia (Mongolia)

Time Period: Late Cretaceous (Campanian to Maastrichtian) 75–71 ma

Size: 5 ft

Much smaller than depicted in movies, *Velociraptor* was a fast and deadly predator. One famous discovery, dubbed the "Fighting Dinosaurs," preserves a *Velociraptor* and *Protoceratops* locked in what appears to be combat, with the *Velociraptor's* sickle claw positioned into the *Protoceratops'* neck. It's thought that the two died when a sudden sandstorm trapped them. Their defining feature is the long, sharp "killing claw" on the hind foot, present in all raptors.

DEINONYCHUS

Pronunciation: dye-NON-ik-us

Meaning: Terrible claw

Lifestyle: Carnivore

Location: North America (USA, Montana, Wyoming, Utah, Oklahoma)

Time Period: Early Cretaceous (Aptian to Albian) 115 -108 ma

Size: 11 ft

Deinonychus teeth have been found with the remains of the plant-eating dinosaur *Tenontosaurus*, which means they may have fed on the large herbivore. *Deinonychus* is important for being the dinosaur that led paleontologists John Ostrom and Robert Bakker to reimagine dinosaurs as fast, nimble, warm-blooded creatures. *Deinonychus*, like all raptors, was covered in feathers, and small knobs on the bones of their forearms called "quill knobs" show they would have had longer, winglike feathers on their arms.

UTAHRAPTOR

Pronunciation: YOO-tah-rap-tor

Meaning: Utah's thief

Lifestyle: Carnivore

Location: North America (Utah)

Time Period: Early Cretaceous (Valanginian to Hauterivian) 135–130 ma

Size: 18 ft

This enormous predator was probably slower and bulkier than its smaller relatives. It had shorter limbs and a stockier build, but with its enormous sickle claw and mouth full of blade-like teeth, it would have been a deadly ambush predator. In 2001, a nine-ton block of sandstone was found in Utah that contained the remains of up to 24 *Utahraptors* of various ages from hatchlings to full-size adults. Also contained within the block were the remains of the large herbivore *Hippodraco*. It's believed that *Hippodraco* got mired in quicksand and was fed upon by the *Utahraptors*, who subsequently became trapped and died themselves.

DAKOTARAPTOR

Pronunciation: dah-KOW-tah-RAP-tor

Meaning: Dakota's thief

Lifestyle: Carnivore

Location: North America (USA, South Dakota)

Time Period: Late Cretaceous (Maastrichtian) 68–66 ma

Size: 18 ft

Similar in size to *Utahraptor*, *Dakotaraptor* lived much later at the end of the Cretaceous Period. Its discovery showed that giant raptors survived right up until the extinction event that killed off the nonavian dinosaurs.

ALLOSAURUS

Pronunciation: AL-uh-SAWR-us

Meaning: Different lizard

Lifestyle: Carnivore

Location: North America (USA, Colorado, Wyoming, Utah, Texas)

Time Period: Late Jurassic (Kimmeridgian to Tithonian) 155–145 ma

Size: 28 ft

This fearsome predator featured huge, hooked claws on three-fingered hands; jaws with 35 sharp teeth; and a powerful, bulldog-like neck. *Allosaurus* is the most common predator found in the Morrison Formation, where it could have fed on smaller dinosaurs like *Camptosaurus* and even juvenile *Diplodocus* and *Apatosaurus*. Finds from Oklahoma of a giant 35-foot-long predator may be an exceptionally large individual of the species.

YANGCHUANOSAURUS

Pronunciation: yang-chwan-oh-SAWR-us

Meaning: Yangchuan lizard

Lifestyle: Carnivore

Location: Asia (China)

Time Period: Middle to Late Jurassic (Bathonian to Oxfordian) 163–157 ma

Size: 26 ft

Very similar in size and appearance to *Allosaurus, Yangchuanosaurus* would have been the dominant predator in the Shangshaximiao Formation of China. This formation has also yielded the remains of *Mamenchisaurus* and the stegosaurs *Gigantspinosaurus* and *Tuojiangosaurus*. *Yangchuanosaurus* had tall spines along its back, which would have given it a somewhat sail-backed appearance, and a pair of low ridges along its snout.

MEGALOSAURUS

Pronunciation: meh-gah-loh-SAWR-us

Meaning: Great lizard

Lifestyle: Carnivore

Location: Europe (England)

Time Period: Middle Jurassic (Bathonian) 166 ma

Size: 20 ft

Megalosaurus was a medium-size predator that stalked the forests of England during the middle Jurassic. It is notable for being the first nonavian dinosaur to be studied and named in 1824, and for being one of the three dinosaurs (along with *Hylaeosaurus* and *Iguanodon*) on which Sir Richard Owen established the Dinosauria. For a long time, almost all meat-eating dinosaurs were assumed to be *Megalosaurus*. In recent years, this issue has been cleaned up and it is recognized as a valid species.

TORVOSAURUS

Pronunciation: tore-voe-SAWR-us

Meaning: Savage lizard

Lifestyle: Carnivore

Location: North America (USA, Colorado)

Time Period: Late Jurassic (Kimmeridgian) 165 ma

Size: 30 ft

Torvosaurus was a huge, but uncommon, predator in the Morrison Formation. Alongside the slightly smaller and more common *Allosaurus*, it likely would have preyed upon juvenile sauropods and other smaller herbivores like *Camptosaurus*. Additional species of *Torvosaurus* have been found in Portugal, Germany, and possibly Tanzania, England, and Spain, showing it to have been a very widespread genus.

CERATOSAURUS
Pronunciation: ser-AT-oh-SAWR-us

Meaning: Horned lizard

Lifestyle: Carnivore

Location: North America (USA, Colorado)

Time Period: Late Jurassic (Oxfordian to Tithonian) 161–145 ma

Size: 18 ft; possibly up to 23 feet

Ceratosaurus is easily recognizable by the large, blunt horn on its nose and the two horns over its eyes. Along with *Torvosaurus* and *Allosaurus*, it was one of the large predators of the Morrison Formation. Two additional species of *Ceratosaurus* have been described, but it is unclear if these are unique species or if they simply represent different growth stages of the same species.

AUSTRALOVENATOR
Pronunciation: ahs-TRAIL-oh-VEHN-ah-tor

Meaning: Southern hunter

Lifestyle: Carnivore

Location: Australia (Queensland)

Time Period: Late Cretaceous (Cenomanian to Turonian) 95 ma

Size: 20 ft

Australovenator was found in the same location in Australia as the sauropod *Diamintinasaurus*. It was a member of the **megaraptor** family of theropods, a group characterized by huge thumb claws. *Australovenator* was a lightweight, fast dinosaur. In fact, its discoverer referred to it as "the cheetah of the Cretaceous."

CITIPATI

Pronunciation: Sih-tih-PAT-ee

Meaning: Funeral pyre lord

Lifestyle: Omnivore

Location: Asia (Mongolia)

Time Period: Late Cretaceous (Campanian to Maastrichtian) 75–71 ma

Size: 9 ft

Citipati is a typical oviraptor with its short, beaked head; long neck; and very birdlike body. Although no direct feather impressions have been found, it is assumed to have been fully feathered much like a bird. The tall crest on its head seems to vary between individuals and may have been different between males and females, or they may have changed size and shape with age. Fossils of a *Citipati* sitting on its nest and protecting a clutch of eggs have been found.

GIGANTORAPTOR

Pronunciation: jy-GAN-toh-RAP-tor

Meaning: Giant thief

Lifestyle: Omnivore

Location: Asia (Mongolia)

Time Period: Late Cretaceous (Cenomanian) 96 ma

Size: 26 ft

All the known oviraptors were relatively small dinosaurs, but *Gigantoraptor* stretched to nearly three times the size of others in the group. This was a gigantic dinosaur with a large head and a blunt, toothless beak. The oviraptors, including *Gigantoraptor*, were likely omnivores, meaning they ate both plants and meat. A clutch of 26 large oval eggs up to 24 inches long discovered in Mongolia have been unofficially assigned to *Gigantoraptor*.

FALCARIUS

Pronunciation: fahl-KEHR-ee-us

Meaning: Sickle cutter

Lifestyle: Omnivore (?)

Location: North America (USA, Utah)

Time Period: Early Cretaceous (Valanginian) 139–134 ma

Size: 16 ft

Falcarius is known from several specimens ranging in age. It's been described as "the ultimate in bizarre: a cross between an ostrich, a gorilla, and Edward Scissorhands." This, along with *Martharaptor* (which is a therizinosaur despite its "raptor" name) are the only two therizinosaurs currently known from North America. Its presence this early in the Cretaceous is important in showing that the therizinosaurs had become widespread by this time.

BEIPIAOSAURUS

Pronunciation: bay-PEE-ow-SAWR-us

Meaning: Beipiao lizard

Lifestyle: Herbivore (?)

Location: Asia (China)

Time Period: Early Cretaceous (Aptian) 125 ma

Size: 7.2 ft

Beiapiaosaurus is from the famed Yixian Formation in China that has given us the most remarkable fossils of birds and feathered dinosaurs. All the specimens discovered have feather impressions. This was a relatively small therizinosaur, but it had a relatively larger head than others in the group. Analysis of the feather impressions imply that it was brownish in color.

THERIZINOSAURUS

Pronunciation: THER-ih-zin-oh-SAWR-us

Meaning: Scythe lizard

Lifestyle: Omnivore (?)

Location: Asia (Mongolia)

Time Period: Early Cretaceous (Maastrichtian) 70 ma

Size: 33 ft

All we really know of *Therizinosaurus* are its arms, hands, shoulders, and a few rib bones. Its overall appearance is based on much smaller relatives. It lived alongside the equally huge and weird ornithomimid, *Deinocheirus*, at a site in Mongolia known as the Nemegt Formation. Its most striking features are its huge claws that were more than 20 inches long. Though threatening in appearance, research has shown that the claws were rather flimsy and could not have been used to attack other dinosaurs. They were most likely used as a threat to scare off potential threats, or as a display to attract mates.

DILONG

Pronunciation: DEE-lohng

Meaning: Emperor dragon

Lifestyle: Carnivore

Location: Asia (China)

Time Period: Early Cretaceous (Aptian) 125 ma

Size: 6.6 ft

We think of tyrannosaurs as giant predators like *T-rex*, but they started out as small, insignificant predators in the late Jurassic and early Cretaceous. This little predator would have hunted among the many feathered dinosaurs known from the Yixian Formation in China. Like most primitive tyrannosaurs, *Dilong* had three-fingered hands rather than the two fingers we see in the later, more advanced tyrannosaurs. We know that *Dilong* was covered in protofeathers, as they're preserved in the fossil remains.

YUTYRANNUS

Pronunciation: YOO-tie-RAN-us

Meaning: Feathered tyrant

Lifestyle: Carnivore

Location: Asia (China)

Time Period: Early Cretaceous (Aptian) 125 ma

Size: 29.5 ft

Yutyrannus is the largest known meat-eating dinosaur to have evidence of having been covered in protofeathers. The protofeathers were long, up to 20 centimeters in length, which would have given *Yutyrannus* a shaggy appearance. *Yutyrannus* is considered a primitive tyrannosaur because it still had three-fingered hands and some other primitive physical traits. Many researchers believe that the later, more advanced tyrannosaurs shed their protofeather coverings as adults and only had them as babies and juveniles.

TYRANNOSAURUS REX

Pronunciation: tye-RAN-uh-SAWR-us

Meaning: Tyrant lizard king

Lifestyle: Carnivore

Location: North America (USA, North and South Dakota, Montana, Wyoming, Colorado)

Time Period: Late Cretaceous (Maastrichtian) 68–66 ma

Size: 46 ft

Inarguably the most popular and best-known dinosaur, *T-rex* as it's come to be known, has earned its reputation as a fearsome predator. Heavier and even more massive than its depiction in popular movies, *T-rex* was an effective ambush predator. *Tyrannosaurus* teeth marks found on the bones of *Triceratops* and *Edmontosaurus* prove they were a food source, but we can't say whether *T-rex* hunted them or scavenged their dead carcasses. There's no evidence that *T-rex* was feathered; however, many researchers believe it was covered in protofeathers, likely as a juvenile.

TARBOSAURUS

Pronunciation: tar-boe-SAWR-us

Meaning: Alarming lizard

Lifestyle: Carnivore

Location: Asia (Mongolia)

Time Period: Late Cretaceous (Maastrichtian) 70 ma

Size: 33 ft

Tarbosaurus was closely related to T-rex but was smaller and more lightly built. In fact, it is so like *T-rex* that some researchers believe it should be a species of *Tyrannosaurus (Tyrannosaurus bataar)*, rather than a distinct genus. It also lived a few million years earlier than *T-rex*, and in Asia.

DASPLETOSAURUS

Pronunciation: das-PLEET-oh-SAWR-us

Meaning: Frightful lizard

Lifestyle: Carnivore

Location: North America (Canada, Alberta; USA, Montana)

Time Period: Late Cretaceous (Campanian) 77–74 ma

Size: 30 ft

Daspletosaurus was a typical advanced tyrannosaur, with two-fingered hands, a large head, and massive teeth. Like all other advanced tyrannosaurs, it also had binocular vision. This means that it could perceive depth, which is a great advantage if you're a predator. It lived at the same time and place as another large tyrannosaur, *Gorgosaurus*, and researchers believe that they may have fed in different areas, or on different food sources.

ALBERTOSAURUS

Pronunciation: Al-bur-toe-SAWR-us

Meaning: Alberta lizard

Lifestyle: Carnivore

Location: North America (Canada, Alberta)

Time Period: Late Cretaceous (Maastrichtian) 71–68 ma

Size: 30 ft

The remains of several *Albertosaurus* have been found together in what appears to be a single death event. This could mean that they lived together as a family group or pack. It could also mean that their bodies were brought together after dying in a flood or other natural disaster. We can't be completely sure, but it does point to gregarious or social behavior and is important in giving us clues about how these dinosaurs lived.

LYTHRONAX

Pronunciation: LYE-thrown-ax

Meaning: Gore king

Lifestyle: Carnivore

Location: North America (USA, Utah)

Time Period: Late Cretaceous (Campanian) 81 ma

Size: 26 ft

Lythronax is the oldest advanced tyrannosaur we know from North America, having lived about 10 million years earlier than any others. Its discovery shed light on how tyrannosaurs evolved and populated North America near the end of the Cretaceous. Its remains were found in the Wahweap Formation in Utah, a site that has produced the remains of several new dinosaur species over the past 15–20 years, including several new horned dinosaurs.

ALIORAMUS

Pronunciation: al-ee-oh-RAY-muhs

Meaning: Different branch

Lifestyle: Carnivore

Location: Asia (Mongolia)

Time Period: Late Cretaceous (Maastrichtian) 70 ma

Size: 20 ft

Alioramus represents a unique branch of late tyrannosaurs that were smaller and had heads that were shaped differently from other tyrannosaurs. Most late tyrannosaurs had massive skulls with blunt, rounded snouts. *Alioramus* and its close relative *Quianzhousaurus* had long, thin, pointed snouts. *Alioramus* lived at the same time and place as *Tarbosaurus*. Some researchers believe that *Alioramus* could be a juvenile *Tarbosaurus*, but this is not widely accepted.

NANUQSAURUS

Pronunciation: nah-NOOK-sawr-us

Meaning: Polar bear lizard

Lifestyle: Carnivore

Location: North America (USA, Alaska)

Time Period: Late Cretaceous (Maastrichtian) 70–68 ma

Size: 20 ft

This small tyrannosaur is most notable for where it was found—in Alaska, north of the Arctic circle. Temperatures in the late Cretaceous were warmer than they are now, but the area was far enough north that it would have been quite cool, and it likely snowed at times during the year. The presence of dinosaurs in Alaska supports the idea of some dinosaurs being warm-blooded, or of having some internal (biological) way of retaining their body temperature in such cool conditions.

STRUTHIOMIMUS

Pronunciation: stroo-thee-oh-MY-muhs

Meaning: Ostrich mimic

Lifestyle: Omnivore

Location: North America (Canada, Alberta)

Time Period: Late Cretaceous (Campanian to Maastrichtian) 76–66 ma

Size: 14 ft

Struthiomimus is typical of the so-called "Ostrich Dinosaurs." With its long neck, small head, and nimble running legs, it's easy to see how it got its name. All the advanced ornithomimids found have short, toothless beaks, which means they were probably omnivores, feeding on small lizards, amphibians, and mammals, as well as plant material. Feather impressions have been found on dinosaurs closely related to *Struthiomimus*, so it's assumed that it was feathered as well.

DEINOCHEIRUS

Pronunciation: dye-nuh-KYE-rus

Meaning: Horrible hand

Lifestyle: Omnivore

Location: Asia (Mongolia)

Time Period: Early Cretaceous (Maastrichtian) 71–69 ma

Size: 36 ft

This is one of the strangest of all dinosaurs. For decades, *Deinocheirus* was known only from a pair of 8-foot-long arms that had been discovered in Mongolia. When the full skeleton and skull were finally found, they revealed an animal unlike anything previously seen. *Deinocheirus* had a tall sail on its back and a long head. Its toothless beak flared out at the tip like modern spoonbills. And it was huge. At 36 feet long, adults would have been capable of taking on the large tyrannosaurs like *Tarbosaurus* that hunted in the area.

MASSOSPONDYLUS

Pronunciation: mass-oh-SPON-dih-lus

Meaning: Longer vertebrae

Lifestyle: Herbivore

Location: Africa (Lesotho, South Africa, Zimbabwe)

Time Period: Early Jurassic (Hettangian to Pliensbachian) 200–183 ma

Size: 20 ft

Massospondylus was one of the first dinosaurs named and described, in 1854 by the famous dinosaur hunter Sir Richard Owen. It displays the typical prosauropod body with a long neck and tail, hinting at the appearance to come of the later gigantic sauropods. Initially, prosauropods were thought to have been quadrupedal, that is, they walked on all four legs. More recent research has shown them to have been primarily bipedal, and only going down on all fours occasionally.

PLATEOSAURUS

Pronunciation: PLAY-tee-oh-SAWR-us

Meaning: Broad lizard

Lifestyle: Herbivore

Location: Europe (Germany, Switzerland, France, Greenland)

Time Period: Late Triassic (Norian) 227–208 ma

Size: 33 ft

The remains of hundreds of *Plateosaurus* have been found in Germany and across Europe, making it a very well-known dinosaur. One site alone in Germany's Black Forest has yielded the remains of over 100 complete and partial skeletons, that captures a mass death assemblage where the animals got mired in mud, and were later fed on or scavenged by predators.

MAMENCHISAURUS

Pronunciation: mah-men-chih-SAWR-us

Meaning: Mamenchi lizard

Lifestyle: Herbivore

Location: Asia (China)

Time Period: Late Jurassic (Oxfordian) 158–161 ma

Size: 85 but possibly up to 115 ft

The mamenchisaurs are remarkable for the incredibly long necks, which grew from half to two-thirds of their total body length. Several species of *Mamenchisaurus* have been described, with *M. sinocanadorum* being the largest known so far. Its neck alone is estimated to have been 39 feet in length.

CETIOSAURUS

Pronunciation: Seh-tee-oh-SAWR-us

Meaning: Whale lizard

Lifestyle: Herbivore

Location: Europe (England, France); Africa (Morocco)

Time Period: Middle Jurassic (Bajocian to Bathonian) 170–166 ma

Size: 52 ft

Cetiosaurus has the distinction of being the first sauropod to have been named in 1842 by Sir Richard Own. He named it "whale lizard" because, at the time it was discovered, the bones were so large he thought they had to have come from some giant, extinct crocodile. He also noticed that the backbones were similar to those of whales, hence its name. For a long time, all sauropod bones found in Europe were thought to belong to *Cetiosaurus*, so it became a "wastebasket genus" until late in the 20th century.

ATLASAURUS
Pronunciation: AT-lah-SAWR-us

Meaning: Atlas lizard

Lifestyle: Herbivore

Location: Africa (Morocco)

Time Period: Middle Jurassic (Bathonian to Callovian) 167–164 ma

Size: 49 ft

This unique sauropod had very different proportions than most members of the group, with a shorter neck and larger head. It's rare to find the skulls of sauropods among their remains—the bones of the skull are very thin and delicate and don't preserve well. The discoverers of *Atlasaurus* were lucky to have found a nearly complete skeleton with the skull, giving us a very good idea of what it looked like.

SHUNOSAURUS
Pronunciation: shoo-noe-SAWR-us

Meaning: Shu lizard

Lifestyle: Herbivore

Location: Asia (China)

Time Period: Late Jurassic (Oxfordian) 159 ma

Size: 36 ft

Shunosaurus is one of a few sauropods that have been discovered with a tail club. Others include *Mamenchisaurus* and *Spinophorosaurus*. *Shunosaurus's* club consisted of an oval mass of bone studded with four spikes. This was apparently used as a weapon that could have been swung at attacking meat eaters.

APATOSAURUS

Pronunciation: ah-PAT-uh-SAWR-us

Meaning: Deceptive lizard

Lifestyle: Herbivore

Location: North America (USA, Colorado, Wyoming, New Mexico, Oklahoma, Utah)

Time Period: Late Jurassic (Kimmeridgian to Tithonian) 152–150 ma

Size: 75 ft

Apatosaurus is the "typical" sauropod familiar to most people. Long known as *Brontosaurus*, that name fell out of favor in the last half of the 20th century. Recent research, however, has revived the name and assigned it to what was once considered a species of *Apatosaurus* (now known as *Brontosaurus excelsus*). It's all very confusing, though not uncommon in paleontology, where new research methods may reverse previous findings.

BAROSAURUS

Pronunciation: bahr-oh-SAWR-us

Meaning: Heavy lizard

Lifestyle: Herbivore

Location: North America (USA, Utah, South Dakota, Colorado, Oklahoma, Wyoming)

Time Period: Late Jurassic (Tithonian) 152–150 ma

Size: 89 ft

Barosaurus lived in what is now the Morrison Formation alongside many better-known sauropods, including *Apatosaurus, Brontosaurus, Diplodocus,* and *Brachiosaurus. Barosaurus* had a relatively longer neck than its diplodocid cousins and, despite its name meaning, was a more lightly built animal overall.

DIPLODOCUS

Pronunciation: dih-PLOD-uh-kus

Meaning: Double beam

Lifestyle: Herbivore

Location: North America (USA, Wyoming, Colorado, Montana, Utah)

Time Period: Late Jurassic (Kimmeridgian) 154–152 ma

Size: 85 ft and up to 95 feet

Diplodocus is one of the most complete large sauropods that has been discovered, and casts of its skeleton are familiar to museumgoers around the world. A diplodocus nicknamed "Dippy" is the star attraction of the Museum of Natural History in London. There are currently two valid species. Originally called *Seismosaurus, D. hallorum* was originally reported to have been up to 152 feet in length. This has since been scaled back to a maximum size of around 95 feet.

SUPERSAURUS

Pronunciation: soo-per-SAWR-us

Meaning: Super lizard

Lifestyle: Herbivore

Location: North America (USA, Colorado, Wyoming)

Time Period: Late Jurassic (Tithonian) 153–145 ma

Size: 110 ft

The history of *Supersaurus* is riddled with confusion. At one time it was considered a very large specimen of *Diplodocus*. Later, a dinosaur that was once named *Ultrasauros* turned out to be a combination of *Supersaurus* and *Brachiosaurus*. To date, *Supersaurus* is the largest known of the many sauropods discovered in the Morrison Formation and one of the largest-known sauropods overall.

NIGERSAURUS

Pronunciation: NEE-jer-SAWR-us

Meaning: Niger lizard

Lifestyle: Herbivore

Location: Africa (Niger)

Time Period: Early Cretaceous (Aptian to Albian) 115–105 ma

Size: 30 ft

Nigersaurus belongs to a line of sauropods called the rebbachi-saurids that are known from the early Cretaceous. *Nigersaurus* is unique among sauropods in that it had a dental battery—hundreds of small teeth that form a chewing surface. Dental batteries are well-known in duckbill and horned dinosaurs, but *Nigersaurus* is the only known sauropod to possess one.

BRACHYTRACHELOPAN

Pronunciation:
brak-ee-trak-ehl-OH-pan

Meaning: Short-necked Pan

Lifestyle: Herbivore

Location: South America (Argentina)

Time Period: Late Jurassic (Oxfordian to Tithonian) 160–150 ma

Size: 35 ft

This small sauropod has a very short neck (the shortest of any known sauropod). It was found in the Cañadón Cálcero Formation in southern Argentina and shared its environment with an as-yet-undescribed, large predator and another sauropod. Exactly how and why it evolved such a short neck is unclear, but it likely helped facilitate browsing on low-growing plants and ferns.

DICRAEOSAURUS

Pronunciation: dye-KRAY-ohSAWR-us

Meaning: Double-forked lizard

Lifestyle: Herbivore

Location: Africa (Tanzania)

Time Period: Late Jurassic (Kimmeridgian to Tithonian) 155–150 ma

Size: 49 ft

The dicraeosaurs are known for their split or bifurcated neck and back spines. In the case of *Dicraeosaurus*, this created a low sail along its back. This was the first of the dicraeosaurs to be recognized, and the group takes its name from this genus. *Dicraeosaurus* was found in the Tendaguru Formation of Tanzania in Africa, which was also home to the stegosaur *Kentrosaurus* and the macronarian sauropod *Giraffatitan*.

AMARGASAURUS

Pronunciation: ah-MAHR-goh-SAWR-us

Meaning: La Amarga lizard

Lifestyle: Herbivore

Location: South America (Argentina)

Time Period: Early Cretaceous (Barremian to Aptian) 129–122 ma

Size: 43 ft

Amargasaurus had extremely long neck and back spines that stretched backward. There's been much debate about how these may have appeared in life. Originally it was assumed these would have been covered in thin skin, creating a double sail along its neck. Later researchers believed the spines were free of skin and may have been used to make sounds by rubbing or clacking them together. The latest thinking is that they were covered in thicker, more muscular skin, creating a single hump down its neck and back.

CAMARASAURUS

Pronunciation: kuh-MARE-uh-SAWR-us

Meaning: Chamber lizard

Lifestyle: Herbivore

Location: North America (USA, Wyoming, Montana, New Mexico, Colorado, Utah)

Time Period: Late Jurassic (Kimmeridgian to Tithonian) 155–145 ma

Size: 75 ft

The macronarians are a line of sauropods with tall arched nose bones that created a helmeted appearance. *Camarasaurus* was one of the most common sauropod dinosaurs in the Morrison Formation of the western United States during the late Jurassic. Several skeletons have been found, including those of juveniles. For a long time, it was believed that macronarians had their nostrils way back on top of their heads. It's now believed that they were positioned at the ends of their snouts.

GIRAFFATITAN

Pronunciation: ger-AF-uh-TYE-ten

Meaning: Giraffe titan

Lifestyle: Herbivore

Location: Africa (Tanzania)

Time Period: Late Jurassic (Tithonian) 150–145 ma

Size: 75 ft

This is the animal most people recognize as *Brachiosaurus*. In fact, it was named *Brachiosaurus* until 1991 when it was recognized that this animal, upon which most reconstructions of *Brachiosaurus* were based, was different enough to be put in its own separate genus, and it was renamed *Giraffatitan*. *Giraffatitan* was part of the Tendaguru Formation, which included the stegosaur *Kentrosaurus*.

EUROPASAURUS

Pronunciation: yoo-ROWP-ah-SAWR-us

Meaning: European lizard

Lifestyle: Herbivore

Location: Europe (Germany)

Time Period: Late Jurassic (Kimmeridgian) 154 ma

Size: 20 ft

Europasaurus looked like a miniature *Giraffatitan*, and in many ways, it was. It featured the same very tall nose bones, but adults grew to only 20 feet long. This is assumed to be the result of a condition called insular dwarfism, where animals that live on islands evolve to a smaller size because of the limited natural resources. Europe in the late Jurassic was not a full continent but a series of small, isolated islands.

SAUROPOSEIDON

Pronunciation: sahr-oh-poe-SYE-don

Meaning: Lizard earthquake god

Lifestyle: Herbivore

Location: North America (USA, Texas, Oklahoma, Wyoming)

Time Period: Early Cretaceous (Aptian to Albian) 118–110 ma

Size: 89–112 ft

This was a huge dinosaur, but it's only known from a few neck bones. If it was built like *Giraffatitan* (which we assume it was), its neck might have reached 60 feet in the air. *Sauroposeidon* is one of the last sauropods to live in North America before the so-called "sauropod hiatus," a period of some 20–25 million years in the middle of the Cretaceous during which there's no evidence of sauropods on the continent.

ARGENTINOSAURUS

Pronunciation:
AHR-gen-TEEN-uh-SAWR-us

Meaning: Argentina lizard

Lifestyle: Herbivore

Location: South America (Argentina)

Time Period: Late Cretaceous (Cenomanian to Turonian) 96–92 ma

Size: 115 ft

Long considered the largest land animal to have ever lived, we now know that there were several titanosaurs around the size of *Argentinosaurus*. South America was where these massive animals were most common, with several species such *Puertasaurus* having been found there, but equally gigantic animals have been discovered in Egypt, North America, and India. Regardless of whether it was the biggest, *Argentinosaurus* was a massive animal that may have reached 80–100 tons in mass.

SALTASAURUS

Pronunciation: sahl-tah-SAWR-us

Meaning: Salta lizard

Lifestyle: Herbivore

Location: South America (Argentina)

Time Period: Late Cretaceous (Maastrichtian) 70–68 ma

Size: 28 ft

Small for a titanosaur, *Saltasaurus* is one of several titanosaurs known to have possessed osteoderms, bony plates that embedded in the skin like those seen in stegosaurs and ankylosaurs. Scientists have also found a *Saltasaurus* nesting site at a location called Auca Mahuevo in Argentina with nests containing fossilized eggs 4–5 inches in diameter, some of which contain fossilized embryos.

PATAGOTITAN

Pronunciation: pah-TAY-goh-tye-tan

Meaning: Patagonia titan

Lifestyle: Herbivore

Location: South America (Argentina)

Time Period: Early Cretaceous (Albian) 101 ma

Size: 102 ft

Another South American giant, *Patagotitan* was heralded as the largest land animal to have ever lived by its discoverers. Later analysis found that it was somewhat smaller than initially thought, though at 102 feet and up to 63 tons, it was still a massive animal. *Patagotitan* is one of the most completely known of the giant titanosaurs, with six individuals having been found at the same site.

LESOTHOSAURUS

Pronunciation: leh-soh-thoh-SAWR-us

Meaning: Lesotho lizard

Lifestyle: Herbivore

Location: Africa (Lesotho)

Time Period: Early Jurassic (Sinemurian) 199–190 ma

Size: 6.6 ft

Lesothosaurus is one of the earliest known ornithischians. The upper Elliot Formation where it was found is known for its large number of small, primitive, plant-eating dinosaurs, with at least seven different species found so far. Some researchers believe *Lesothosaurus* may be one of the earliest and most primitive members of the thyreophorans, the group of armored dinosaurs that includes stegosaurs and ankylosaurs, though this is not widely accepted.

HYPSILOPHODON

Pronunciation: hip-sil-AWE-foe-dawn

Meaning: Hypsilophus tooth

Lifestyle: Herbivore, possibly omnivore

Location: Europe (England)

Time Period: Early Cretaceous (Barremian) 130–125 ma

Size: 6.6 ft

Hypsilophodon shows the traits typical of small plant-eating dinosaurs found all over the world. While not as flashy as the stegosaurs or ankylosaurs, these little animals were critical in their ecosystems, providing an important food source to medium- and large-size predators. All these little ornithischians looked very similar, with long back legs well suited for running, shorter front legs, and small heads.

THESCELOSAURUS

Pronunciation: thes-kehl-oh-SAWR-us

Meaning: Wondrous lizard

Lifestyle: Herbivore

Location: North America (USA, Wyoming, Montana, Colorado; Canada, Alberta)

Time Period: Late Cretaceous (Maastrichtian) 68–66 ma

Size: 13 ft

One of the larger ornithischians, *Thescelosaurus* lived at the end of the Mesozoic and shared its environment with the predators *Tyrannosaurus* and *Dakotaraptor*. It also appears to have been a common dinosaur in its environment. Based on the proportions of its leg bones, *Thescelosaurus* was probably not as fast of a runner as most small herbivores.

WEEWARRASAURUS

Pronunciation: wee-WAHR-oh-SAWR-us

Meaning: Wee Wara lizard

Lifestyle: Herbivore

Location: Australia

Time Period: Late Cretaceous (Cenomanian) 100–93 ma

Size: 6–8 ft

Weewarrasaurus is notable because its fossils were opalized. The Griman Creek Formation in Australia is known for its opal mines, and many fossils, including fossilized pine cones and animal bones, have become preserved as opal. The area is also known for having a lot of different small, plant-eating dinosaurs that lived together.

IGUANODON

Pronunciation: ih-GWAHN-oh-don

Meaning: Iguana tooth

Lifestyle: Herbivore

Location: Europe (England, Belgium, Germany, Spain)

Time Period: Early Cretaceous (Barremian) 126–122 ma

Size: 30 ft (possibly larger)

Iguanodon is a well-known dinosaur, with several fossils having been found over the years. It probably spent most of its time walking on all fours, rearing up on its back legs to feed off higher foliage. *Iguanodon's* thumb evolved into a large spike, the purpose of which is unclear. It may have been used like a hook to grasp vegetation, or it may have been used as a weapon against predators. *Iguanodon* was one of the first dinosaurs to be studied and named.

CAMPTOSAURUS

Pronunciation: KAMP-tuh-SAWR-us

Meaning: Flexible lizard

Lifestyle: Herbivore

Location: North America (USA, Wyoming)

Time Period: Late Jurassic (Callovian to Oxfordian) 156–146 ma

Size: 20 ft

This medium-size herbivore might have scampered between the legs of the giant sauropods that were common in the Morrison Formation of the western USA in the late Jurassic. Facing off against predators like *Allosaurus* and *Ceratosaurus, Camptosaurus* would have had little means of defense other than to try and run away. *Camptosaurus* did not have a thumb spike like many other iguanodonts, but instead had five fingers on its hand.

MUTTABURRASAURUS
Pronunciation:
MUH-tuh-burr-ah-SAWR-us

Meaning: Muttaburra lizard

Lifestyle: Herbivore

Location: Australia (Queensland)

Time Period: Early Cretaceous (Albian) 112–103 ma

Size: 26 ft

The remains of *Muttaburrasaurus* are the most complete of any Australian dinosaur. This large herbivore was likely bipedal, only going down on all fours occasionally to graze or drink. The end of its snout flared out into a large, arching muzzle, which may have been used to make calls or for display purposes.

HIPPODRACO
Pronunciation: hih-poe-DRAY-koe

Meaning: Horse dragon

Lifestyle: Herbivore

Location: North America (USA, Utah)

Time Period: Late Cretaceous (Valanginian) 139–134 ma

Size: 15 ft

The Cedar Mountain Formation, where *Hippodraco* was discovered, is one of the most productive sites in North America for early Jurassic dinosaur remains. *Hippodraco* would have shared its environment with the ankylosaur *Gastonia* and the giant dromaeosaur *Utahraptor*. A skeleton of *Hippodraco* was found in a huge block of sandstone with several *Utahraptor* skeletons that appear to have been feasting on the herbivore when they got caught in quicksand.

TENONTOSAURUS

Pronunciation: ten-on-toe-SAWR-us

Meaning: Sinew lizard

Lifestyle: Herbivore

Location: North America (USA, Wyoming, Texas, Utah, Idaho, possibly Maryland)

Time Period: Early Cretaceous (Aptian to Albian) 115–108 ma

Size: 23 ft

This seemingly unremarkable ornithopod was one of the most common dinosaurs during the early Cretaceous of North America. Its remains are often found associated with the teeth of meat-eating dinosaurs like *Deinonychus*, implying that it was a frequent food source. The exact classification of *Tenontosaurus* has been controversial, with some researchers labeling it an iguanodont and others an extremely large hypsilophodontid.

OURANOSAURUS

Pronunciation: oor-ahn-oh-SAWR-us

Meaning: Brave lizard

Lifestyle: Herbivore

Location: Africa (Niger)

Time Period: Early Cretaceous (Aptian to Albian) 121–113 ma

Size: 27 ft

Ouranosaurus is another dinosaur that evolved long back spines, forming a tall sail. It's also an example of a dinosaur whose classification has changed a few times over the years, as it shows physical traits that are known from both iguanodontids (a large thumb spike) and hadrosaurs. *Ouranosaurus* lived at the same time as the giant crocodilian *Sarcosuchus* and may have been its prey.

SCUTELLOSAURUS

Pronunciation: skoo-tell-oh-SAWR-us

Meaning: Little shield lizard

Lifestyle: Herbivore

Location: North America (USA, Arizona)

Time Period: Early Jurassic (Sinemurian) 196 ma

Size: 4.3 ft

Tiny *Scutellosaurus* was one of the earliest and most primitive of the armored dinosaurs. It was a lightly armored, bipedal plant eater that looked very much like the primitive ornithischians from which it evolved. *Scutellosaurus* was a fast runner, and it needed to be, in order to escape the large predators like *Dilophosaurus* that lived alongside it.

SCELIDOSAURUS

Pronunciation: skeh-LIHD-oh-SAWR-us

Meaning: Limb lizard

Lifestyle: Herbivore

Location: Europe (England)

Time Period: Early Jurassic (Sinemurian to Pliensbachian) 195–183 ma

Size: 13 ft

Scelidosaurus is the earliest large-bodied armored dinosaur found so far. It was also one of the first dinosaurs discovered (in 1859) and was named by Sir Richard Owen. The armor on *Scelidosaurus* was simple compared to later thyreophorans, consisting of rows of bony scutes. It did not have a tail club or spikes like the later ankylosaurs and stegosaurs.

JAKAPIL

Pronunciation: JAH-kah-pill

Meaning: Shield bearer

Lifestyle: Herbivore

Location: South America (Argentina)

Time Period: Late Cretaceous (Cenomanian) 97–94 ma

Size: 4.9 ft

When the discovery of *Jakapil* was announced in 2022, it caused a bit of a sensation in the world of paleontology. Though it was clearly a thyreophoran, it stood on two legs and a body unlike any other thyreophoran discovered. This little dinosaur would have scampered about in the underbrush, trying to avoid being a snack for *Giganotosaurus*.

ANKYLOSAURUS

Pronunciation: AN-kye-loe-SAWR-us

Meaning: Fused or bent lizard

Lifestyle: Herbivore

Location: North America (USA, Montana, Wyoming, New Mexico; Canada, Alberta)

Time Period: Late Cretaceous (Maastrichtian) 68–66 ma

Size: 26 ft

The best known of the ankylosaurs was also one of the last surviving members of the group. *Ankylosaurus* is the largest ankylosaur known so far, reaching lengths of up to 26 feet. With its massive tail club and heavily armored body, it would have been a formidable rival of *Tyrannosaurus rex* that shared its environment. The exact arrangement of its armor has been a subject of debate. It does not appear to have had spikes along its sides (though it's often depicted this way), and agreement on how the plates on its back were arranged has changed as new researchers have studied it.

SAICHANIA

Pronunciation: say-KAN-ee-ah

Meaning: Beautiful one

Lifestyle: Herbivore

Location: Asia (Mongolia)

Time Period: Late Cretaceous (Campanian) 75–70 ma

Size: 22 ft

Saichania was a heavily armored ankylosaur that shared its habitat with other ankylosaurs, including *Tarchia* and *Zaraapelta*. The Barun Goyot Formation, where its remains were found, preserve a desert environment of sand dunes and oases, but it must have contained enough low-growing vegetation to support a vast array of large-bodied plant eaters.

EUOPLOCEPHALUS

Pronunciation: yoo-oh-ploe-seff-ah-luhs

Meaning: Well-armored head

Lifestyle: Herbivore

Location: North America (Canada, Alberta)

Time Period: Late Cretaceous (Campanian) 76–75 ma

Size: 17 ft

For a long time, many ankylosaur remains found throughout North America were attributed to *Euoplocephalus*. In the late 20th century, new research identified many of those remains as different species. *Euoplocephalus* lived in what is now the Dinosaur Park Formation in Canada and shared its environment with many duckbills and horned dinosaurs. It may have been preyed upon by the tyrannosaurs *Albertosaurus* and *Daspletosaurus*.

ZUUL

Pronunciation: zool

Meaning: From the character Zuul

Lifestyle: Herbivore

Location: North America (USA, Montana)

Time Period: Late Cretaceous (Campanian) 75 ma

Size: 20 ft

Named after the demon in the film *Ghostbusters*, the remains of *Zuul* were found in the Judith River Formation of Montana. *Zuul* is noteworthy for sporting one of the largest tail clubs known for ankylosaurs. In a very rare occurance, the fossil of *Zuul* also preserved remnants of scales—not skin impressions, but actual remains of the skin tissue.

STEGOUROS

Pronunciation: steh-GOO-rows

Meaning: Roofed tail

Lifestyle: Herbivore

Location: South America (Chile)

Time Period: Late Cretaceous (Maastrichtian) 74–71 ma

Size: 6.6 ft

South America has yielded some of the most unusual thyreophorans (see *Jakapil*, p. 112). *Stegouros* is unique not only for its small size but also for its unusual tail club, which was formed from a series of sharpened fused plates that spread out from the tail center. The environment of the Dorotea Formation in Chile where it was found appears to have been a shoreline, as many marine reptiles have been discovered in the same formation.

GARGOYLEOSAURUS

Pronunciation:
Gar-goy-lee-oh-SAWR-us

Meaning: Gargoyle lizard

Lifestyle: Herbivore

Location: North America (Wyoming)

Time Period: Late Jurassic (Kimmeridgian to Tithonian) 154–150 ma

Size: 11.5 ft

Gargoyleosaurus is among the earliest known ankylosaurs. Its remains were found in the Morrison Formation of the western United States. It would have shared its environment with the enormous sauropods *Apatosaurus, Diplodocus*, and *Brachiosaurus*, and it may have been food for large carnivores like *Ceratosaurus* and *Allosaurus*.

PELOROPLITES

Pronunciation: peh-low-roh-PLYE-tees

Meaning: Monstrous heavy one

Lifestyle: Herbivore

Location: North America (USA, Utah)

Time Period: Late Cretaceous (Cenomanian to Turonian) 98–93 ma

Size: 20 ft

The Cedar Mountain Formation in Utah has produced no less than six different ankylosaurs. So many, in fact, that some researchers have dubbed the early and early late Cretaceous in North America "the age of ankylosaurs." *Peloroplites* was a heavily armored dinosaur with two cervical (neck) rings containing spikes, plus rows of long spikes sticking out from its sides. Like most ankylosaurs, its head was covered in a mosaic of bony osteoderms.

EUROPELTA

Pronunciation: YOO-row-PEHL-tah

Meaning: Europe's shield

Lifestyle: Herbivore

Location: Europe (Spain)

Time Period: Late Cretaceous (Aptian to Albian) 113 ma

Size: 16 ft

Europelta is one of a growing list of European ankylosaurs, which are well represented across several European countries. The location where *Europelta* was discovered also contains significant amounts of charcoal, indicating that the area was subject to wildfires. Whether or not this is what killed *Europelta* is uncertain.

GASTONIA

Pronunciation: gah-STOWN-ee-ah

Meaning: After Rob Gaston

Lifestyle: Herbivore

Location: North America (USA, Utah)

Time Period: Early Cretaceous (Valanginian) 139–125 ma

Size: 20 ft

The Cedar Mountain Formation in Utah is one of the richest sites for early Cretaceous dinosaur remains. The location records an ecosystem of rivers and wetlands that frequently flooded, burying the animals and preserving them. *Gastonia* was one of several nodosaurs that existed at the Cedar Mountain site, and its remains are quite common. Other dinosaurs include the giant raptor *Utahraptor*, the iguanodontid *Hippodraco*, and the therizinosaur *Falcarius*.

BOREALOPELTA

Pronunciation:
BOH-ree-ahl-oh-PEHL-tah

Meaning: Northern shield

Lifestyle: Herbivore

Location: North America (Canada, Alberta)

Time Period: Early Cretaceous (Albian) 113 ma

Size: 18 ft

Borealopelta is a striking, if rather unremarkable, example of a nodosaur. What really makes it spectacular is the state of preservation of its fossil. *Borealopelta* is the best-preserved dinosaur ever found. The state of preservation is so complete that researchers have identified soft tissues such as skin and keratin (that are almost never preserved), as well as internal organs and the remains of its last meal, which showed that it ate leaves, ferns, and twigs.

STEGOSAURUS

Pronunciation: STEG-uh-SAWR-us

Meaning: Roofed lizard

Lifestyle: Herbivore

Location: North America (USA, Colorado, Montana, Oklahoma, Utah, Wyoming)

Time Period: Late Jurassic (Kimmeridgian to Tithonian) 155–145 ma

Size: 21 ft

This well-known and popular dinosaur is found in the Morrison Formation of the western United States. For a long time, it was reported that *Stegosaurus* had a second brain located in its hip to help control the movement of its tail. This isn't true. Researchers still debate the purpose of the tall plates along its back. They may have helped regulate body temperature, they may have been used to defend itself against predators, attract mates, or intimidate rivals. Its tail spikes, known as its **thagomizer,** were clearly used to defend itself against predatory dinosaurs like *Allosaurus* and *Ceratosaurus*.

GIGANTSPINOSAURUS

Pronunciation: Jye-gant-spy-no-SAWR-us

Meaning: Giant spined lizard

Lifestyle: Herbivore

Location: Asia (China)

Time Period: Late Jurassic (Oxfordian) 165 ma

Size: 14 ft

What sets *Gigantspinosaurus* apart from other stegosaurs is its enormous shoulder spikes. Their purpose is unclear, but they would have provided effective defense against predators.

KENTROSAURUS

Pronunciation: KEN-troh-SAWR-us

Meaning: Prickle lizard

Lifestyle: Herbivore

Location: Africa (Tanzania)

Time Period: Late Jurassic (Tithonian) 152 ma

Size: 15 ft

The remains of *Kentrosaurus* were found in the Tendaguru Formation in Tanzania. The dinosaur fauna discovered there is very similar to the Morrison Formation in the western United States, consisting of stegosaurs, allosaurus, and large sauropods. The spikes and plates of *Kentrosaurus* were especially long, making it look like a walking pin cushion, hence its name.

MIRAGAIA

Pronunciation: MEER-uh-guy-EE-uh

Meaning: Named after Miragaia, the location where it was found

Lifestyle: Herbivore

Location: Europe (Portugal)

Time Period: Late Jurassic (Kimmeridgian to Tithonian) 150 ma

Size: 21 ft

The most notable feature of *Miragaia* is its long neck, nearly twice as long as those of other stegosaurs. This has led some researchers to describe it as the "sauropod stegosaur." It achieved that long length not by stretching out the length of each neck vertebrae, but rather by adding more vertebrae to its neck—a total of 17, the most known of any stegosaur.

EOTRACHODON

Pronunciation: EE-oh-TRAK-oh-dahn

Meaning: Dawn Trachodon

Lifestyle: Herbivore

Location: North America (USA, Alabama)

Time Period: Late Cretaceous (Santonian) 86–83 ma

Size: 19–24 ft

Eotrachodon is unique for a couple of reasons. It's one of the earliest and most primitive hadrosaurs. And it was discovered in the eastern United States, a region with very few dinosaur discoveries. Its discovery, along with a couple of other primitive hadrosaurs from the same area, suggest that Appalachia, as the area was known during the Cretaceous, may have been the ancestral area where hadrosaurs evolved.

TETHYSHADROS

Pronunciation: teth-is-HAD-rose

Meaning: Tethys hadrosaur

Lifestyle: Herbivore

Location: Europe (Italy)

Time Period: Late Cretaceous (Campanian) 81–80 ma

Size: 15 ft

Tethyshadros is one of the few duckbills to be discovered in Europe. It was quite small for a hadrosaur, which may have been the result of insular dwarfism—a condition where animals that live on islands are smaller in size because of the limited resources available to them.

TSINTAOSAURUS

Pronunciation: SIHN-towe-SAWR-us

Meaning: Qingdao lizard

Lifestyle: Herbivore

Location: Asia (China)

Time Period: Late Cretaceous (Campanian) 83–70 ma

Size: 27 ft

When *Tsintaosaurus* was first discovered, it was described as the duckbilled unicorn because it appeared to have a large spike sticking out of the top of its head. Later discoveries showed that this was just a piece of a larger crest that adorned its head.

PARASAUROLOPHUS

Pronunciation:
PAR-ah-sawr-AWL-oh-fus

Meaning: Near-crested lizard

Lifestyle: Herbivore

Location: North America (Canada, Alberta; USA, New Mexico)

Time Period: Late Cretaceous (Campanian) 76–73 ma

Size: 31 ft

Parasaurolophus is one of the most familiar duckbills, thanks to the long crest on top of its head. The exact purpose of the crest has remained a bit of a mystery. It was originally thought that the crest served as a snorkel that allowed it to breath underwater. Now scientists believe that it may have acted as a resonating chamber for sounds and may have been brightly colored and used as display. There are three species of *Parasaurolophus*, all of them bearing tube-like crests of varying sizes.

CORYTHOSAURUS

Pronunciation: coh-RITH-oh-SAWR-us

Meaning: Helmeted lizard

Lifestyle: Herbivore

Location: North America (Canada, Alberta; USA, Montana)

Time Period: Late Cretaceous (Campanian) 77–75 ma

Size: 30 ft

Corythosaurus was one of the first hadrosaurs discovered with skin impressions, giving clues into what the animal looked like when alive. *Corythosaurus* lived at the same time and place as several other crested duckbills, including *Parasaurolophus, Lambeosaurus*, and *Hypacrosaurus*. The presence of all these herbivores would have provided prey for the large tyrannosaurs that stalked the same area.

OLOROTITAN

Pronunciation: OH-loe-roe-TYE-tan

Meaning: Giant swan

Lifestyle: Herbivore

Location: Asia (Russia)

Time Period: Late Cretaceous (Maastrichtian) 72–66 ma

Size: 36 ft

By the end of the Cretaceous, hadrosaurs had spread far across the globe, but the crested hadrosaurs had become extinct in North America, only surviving until the end of the Cretaceous in Asia. *Olorotitan's* crest flared back over its head in a fan shape and was flattened from side to side. *Olorotitan* was so named because its neck, longer than most other hadrosaurs, reminded its discoverers of a swan.

LAMBEOSAURUS

Pronunciation: LAM-bee-oh-SAWR-us

Meaning: Lambe's lizard

Lifestyle: Herbivore

Location: North America (Canada, Alberta; USA, Montana)

Time Period: Late Cretaceous (Campanian) 76–75 ma

Size: 25 ft

Lambeosaurus sported one of the most unusual and dramatic crests of all the duckbills. The front of the crest was a large box-like structure that leaned forward over its nose, while the rear was a long spike that pointed backwards. As with all the crested hadrosaurs, the exact purpose of the crest is unknown. Another species of *Lambeosaurus, L. magnicristatus*, is known that sported a large, forward-pointing helmet-like crest.

BRACHYLOPHOSAURUS

Pronunciation:
BRAK-ee-loff-oh-SAWR-us

Meaning: Short-crested lizard

Lifestyle: Herbivore

Location: North America (Canada, Alberta; USA, Montana, Utah)

Time Period: Late Cretaceous (Campanian) 81–76 ma

Size: 30 ft

The remains of several *Brachylophosaurus* have been found, most notably a mummified individual that has been nicknamed Leonardo. Leonardo is exceptionally well-preserved, with several areas of skin in excellent condition and even the contents of its guts, which showed that it ate leaves, ferns, conifers, and some early flowering plants like magnolias. Despite being one of the "uncrested" hadrosaurs, *Brachylophosaurus* had a small, flat crest on the top of its head.

GRYPOSAURUS

Pronunciation: grip-oh-SAWR-us

Meaning: Hooked-nose lizard

Lifestyle: Herbivore

Location: North America (Canada, Alberta; USA, Montana, Utah)

Time Period: Late Cretaceous (Campanian) 80–75 ma

Size: 26 ft

Gryposaurus and its close relative *Kritosaurus* are easily recognized by the big arching nose that gives it its name. The gryposaurs were a wide-ranging group that populated swamps and marshes from the Gulf of Mexico to Alberta, Canada, during the late Cretaceous.

MAIASAURA

Pronunciation: MY-ah-SAWR-ah

Meaning: Good mother lizard

Lifestyle: Herbivore

Location: North America (Canada, Alberta; USA, Montana)

Time Period: Late Cretaceous (Campanian) 76 ma

Size: 30 ft

Maiasaura looks a lot like its close relative *Brachylophosaurus*, but its discovery marked a milestone in dinosaur research. The name *Maiasaura* ("good mother lizard") refers to the site where it was found, a location known as Egg Mountain. Egg Mountain records a vast nesting colony of *Maiasaura*, with thousands of 15-foot-wide nests spread across a huge area. Within the fossilized nests were the remains of eggs and juveniles, recording the first evidence of parental care in dinosaurs.

SHANTUNGOSAURUS

Pronunciation: shahn-tun-gah-SAWR-us

Meaning: Shantung lizard

Lifestyle: Herbivore

Location: Asia (China)

Time Period: Late Cretaceous (Campanian) 76–73 ma

Size: 49 ft

The largest known hadrosaur was *Shantungosaurus* from China. In appearance, it was very similar to *Edmontosaurus* but much bigger, reaching a size of 50 feet. (That's bigger than *Tyrannosaurus*!) Several *Shantungosaurus* of various sizes and ages were found together at one site, suggesting they may have lived in herds.

EDMONTOSAURUS

Pronunciation: ed-MON-tuh-SAWR-us

Meaning: Royal lizard from Edmonton

Lifestyle: Herbivore

Location: North America (Canada, Alberta; USA, Montana, Wyoming, South Dakota)

Time Period: Late Cretaceous (Campanian) 73 ma

Size: 33 ft

Over the years, *Edmontosaurus* has been known by several different names: *Claosaurus, Trachodon, Anatotitan, Anatosaurus,* and *Thespesius,* among them. Now we recognize all those different names as one genus of dinosaur (with two species). *Edmontosaurus* is the classic "duckbilled" dinosaur and is the dinosaur that gave the group its nickname. *Edmontosaurus regalis* was a bit smaller and its head wasn't quite as flat as its sister species *Edmontosaurus annectens*. It lived about 5–8 million years earlier than *E. annectens.* Several mummified *Edmontosaurus regalis* have been found, including one that shows that it had a soft-tissue, fleshy crest—rather like a rooster's cockscomb.

E. annectens was a bit larger than its earlier relative, *E. regalis*, and its head was lower, flatter, and more, well, duckier. *E. annectens* was one of the last dinosaurs to survive until the end of the Cretaceous, when the extinction of the nonavian dinosaurs occurred. It lived alongside many well-known dinosaurs, including *Triceratops* and *Tyrannosaurus rex.*

YINLONG

Pronunciation: YIHN-long

Meaning: Hidden dragon

Lifestyle: Herbivore

Location: Asia (China)

Time Period: Late Jurassic (Oxfordian) 158 ma

Size: 3.9 ft

One of the first and most primitive of all horned dinosaurs, *Yinlong* looks more like a small ornithischian than the massive horned ceratopsians we're familiar with. A slight expansion at the back of its head would eventually evolve into the massive neck shields seen in later ceratopsians. *Yinlong* also has a small bone at the front of its beak called the rostral bone, which only exists in horned dinosaurs.

PSITTACOSAURUS

Pronunciation: sit-TAK-oh-SAWR-us

Meaning: Parrot lizard

Lifestyle: Herbivore

Location: Asia (China, Mongolia), Europe (Russia)

Time Period: Early Cretaceous (Barremian to Aptian) 125–101 ma

Size: 5 ft

Psittacosaurus is known from hundreds of specimens of all ages—in fact, it's one of the best-known dinosaurs. It's also the dinosaur genus for which the most species have been identified (11 so far). The species pictured is *Psittacosaurus sibericus*. It featured an array of horns and hornlets covering its face and was found in Siberia, Russia. Exceptionally well-preserved remains of another species, *P. mongoliensis*, has shown that it carried a crest of tall fibers along its tail, and that its coloration was darker on top and lighter on the bottom, a pattern known as **counter shading.**

PROTOCERATOPS

Pronunciation: proe-toe-SEHR-ah-tops

Meaning: First horned face

Lifestyle: Herbivore

Location: Asia (China)

Time Period: Late Cretaceous (Campanian to Maastrichtian) 75–71 ma

Size: 8 ft

All the horned dinosaurs had huge heads relative to their bodies, but in *Protoceratops* this was taken to an extreme. Many researchers believe that differences in the size and shape of *Protoceratops* head shields are males and females; however, others believe these differences are just natural variations. *Protoceratops* is a well-known dinosaur with over 100 specimens having been discovered from multiple locations across Mongolia. One famous discovery known as "The Fighting Dinosaurs" records a *Protoceratops* and *Velociraptor* locked in mortal combat.

LEPTOCERATOPS

Pronunciation: LEHP-tow-SEHR-ah-tops

Meaning: Small horned face

Lifestyle: Herbivore

Location: North America (USA, Wyoming; Canada, Alberta)

Time Period: Late Cretaceous (Maastrichtian) 68–66 ma

Size: 6.6 ft

Leptoceratops was similar in size to its relative *Protoceratops* but had a smaller head. It populated the end-Cretaceous forests of North America and may have served as a snack for adult *Tyrannosaurus*. *Leptoceratops* may have been mostly bipedal. A discovery of a *Leptoceratops* bone bed in 2019 showed that they were social animals living in groups, and that they raised their young in burrows.

CENTROSAURUS

Pronunciation: sen-troe-SAWR-us

Meaning: Pointed lizard

Lifestyle: Herbivore

Location: North America (Canada, Alberta)

Time Period: Late Cretaceous (Campanian) 87–75 ma

Size: 16–18 ft

Centrosaurus was a very common dinosaur in its environment. Vast bone beds containing the remains of hundreds of individuals have been found. We've learned a lot about its growth stages from very young to adult specimens. *Centrosaurus's* nose horn and the small hornlets around the rim of its shield varied throughout its age, and even in adults there is a lot of variation, with some nose horns pointing forward, some backwards, and some nearly straight.

STYRACOSAURUS

Pronunciation: stih-RAK-uh-SAWR-us

Meaning: Spiked lizard

Lifestyle: Herbivore

Location: North America (Canada, Alberta)

Time Period: Late Cretaceous (Campanian) 75–74 ma

Size: 16–18 ft

Styracosaurus had a dramatic display of long horns radiating out from the edge of its frill. As with most horned dinosaurs, there was some variation between individuals in the angle and length of the horns. The exact purpose of the horns and frills of horned dinosaurs is still a matter of debate. It seems very likely that they were used as displays to signal potential mates or to help distinguish themselves from other ceratopsians.

DIABLOCERATOPS

Pronunciation: dee-Ab-loe-SEHR-ah-tops

Meaning: Devil-horned face

Lifestyle: Herbivore

Location: North America (USA, Utah)

Time Period: Late Cretaceous (Campanian) 81 ma

Size: 15 ft

Diabloceratops and its close relative *Machairoceratops* represent the earliest and most primitive members of the group in North America. Like all horned dinosaurs, *Diabloceratops* had a sharp beak for cropping plants. It sported two horns over its eyes and had a tall frill, but, unlike most ceratopsians, the frill narrowed at the top and had two forward and outward-curving horns.

SINOCERATOPS

Pronunciation: SYE-noe-SEHR-ah-tops

Meaning: Chinese horned face

Lifestyle: Herbivore

Location: Asia (China)

Time Period: Late Cretaceous (Campanian) 73 ma

Size: 16 ft

Sinoceratops is the only advanced horned dinosaur known from Asia. It had a long horn on its nose and several forward-pointing spikes along the edge of its frill. It was a bit smaller than its depiction in movies, and the large holes in its shield would have been covered with muscle and skin, not open.

PACHYRHINOSAURUS

Pronunciation:
PAK-ee-RYE-noe-SAWR-us

Meaning: Thick-nosed lizard

Lifestyle: Herbivore

Location: North America (USA, Montana, Alaska; Canada, Alberta)

Time Period: Late Cretaceous (Campanian to Maastrichtian) 73–68 ma

Size: 26 ft

Pachyrhinosaurus is another well-known horned dinosaur. Three species of *Pachyrhinosaurus* are known. *P. canadensis* was the largest, reaching lengths of up to 26 feet, and lived around 71 million years ago. Its remains have been found in Canada. *P. lakustai* is the oldest species (73–72 million years ago) and was found in Montana and Canada. *P. perotorum* is the youngest (71-69 million years ago) and was found in Alaska.

TRICERATOPS

Pronunciation: try-SAIR-uh-tops

Meaning: Three-horned face

Lifestyle: Herbivore

Location: North America (USA, Colorado, South Dakota, Wyoming, Montana)

Time Period: Late Cretaceous (Campanian) 68–66 ma

Size: 30 ft

The best-known ceratopsian was also the last known, surviving up to the Cretaceous extinction event. *Triceratops* was the largest ceratopsian, almost twice as long as most. A well-preserved fossil from the Lance Creek Formation in Wyoming, nicknamed Lane, included skin impressions and was covered in large, six-sided scales. Across its back were large pyramid-shaped osteoderms.

KOSMOCERATOPS

Pronunciation:
KAHS-moh-SEHR-ah-tops

Meaning: Ornate horned face

Lifestyle: Herbivore

Location: North America (USA, Utah)

Time Period: Late Cretaceous (Campanian) 76–75 ma

Size: 15 ft

Kosmoceratops is one of several ceratopsians discovered in the Kaiparowits Formation in Utah. Both adults and juveniles were found at the same site. The presence of so many different horned dinosaurs across this region of North America led to speculation that the continent may have been divided into "dinosaur provinces" in which different species evolved in isolation because of geological barriers. *Kosmoceratops* had a fringe of long horns that pointed down and forward from its frill, and two large horns over its eyes pointed outward.

UTAHCERATOPS

Pronunciation: YOO-tah-SEHR-ah-tops

Meaning: Utah horned face

Lifestyle: Herbivore

Location: North America (USA, Utah)

Time Period: Late Cretaceous (Campanian) 76–75 ma

Size: 23 ft

This large ceratopsian was described in 2010. Its remains were found in the fossil-rich Kaiparowits Formation, which has produced the remains of several different ceratopsians. *Utahceratops* is the largest from the area and would have used its sharp beak to crop tough vegetation like cycads and pine trees that largely populated the region.

REGALICERATOPS

Pronunciation:
reh-GAL-oh-SEHR-ah-tops

Meaning: Royal horned face

Lifestyle: Herbivore

Location: North America (Canada, Alberta)

Time Period: Late Cretaceous (Maastrichtian) 68–67 ma

Size: 16 ft

Regaliceratops had a dramatic crown of low spikes all around the edge of its shield, inspiring its name. Nicknamed "Hellboy" by its discoverers (after the popular comic book character), *Regaliceratops* was found in the St. Mary River Formation of Alberta, Canada, by researchers from the famed Royal Tyrell Museum.

PACHYCEPHALOSAURUS

Pronunciation:
PAK-ee-sef-ah-low-SAWR-us

Meaning: Thick-headed lizard

Lifestyle: Herbivore

Location: North America (USA, Montana, Wyoming, South Dakota; Canada, Alberta)

Time Period: Late Cretaceous (Maastrichtian) 68–66 ma

Size: 16 ft

For a long time, pachycephalosaurs were shown butting heads like bighorn sheep. Now it's believed they used their thickened heads to ram into the sides of rivals. Two other pachycephalosaurs that have been found in North America, *Dracorex* and *Stygimoloch*, are considered juvenile versions of *Pachycephalosaurus*. *Pachycephalosaurus* is the largest pachycephalosaur known, reaching two to three times the length of all others.

STEGOCERAS

Pronunciation: STEH-go-SEHR-ahs

Meaning: Horn roof

Lifestyle: Herbivore

Location: North America (Canada, Alberta; USA, Montana, New Mexico)

Time Period: Late Cretaceous (Campanian) 77–74 ma

Size: 6–8 ft

This little dinosaur packed quite a punch with its thickened skull roof rimmed by small knobs and blunted spikes. *Stegoceras* is one of the best-known pachycephalosaurs. All that's been found of most "pachys" is the head dome or (rarely) a full skull. But a nearly complete skeleton of *Stegoceras* has been found, and it formed the basis for what we assume its relatives looked like.

Dinosaurs were the dominant terrestrial life-form during the Mesozoic, but they weren't the only animals. Just like today, the ecosystems of the Mesozoic were filled with all types of animals. Insects swarmed overhead and crawled along the ground. Frogs, salamanders, and other amphibians made their way through swamps. Pterosaurs filled the skies, and mammals scurried about underfoot and burrowed to seek shelter.

Pterosaurs were flying reptiles. While dinosaurs dominated the land in the Mesozoic, pterosaurs ruled the skies. They first appear in the fossil record around the same time as dinosaurs, around 230 million years ago, *but they weren't dinosaurs*. Pterosaurs are a completely different class of reptiles that are only distantly related to dinosaurs. They lived throughout the Mesozoic and went extinct at the same time as dinosaurs, around 66 million years ago. Just like the dinosaurs, pterosaurs started out as small creatures less than a meter in wingspan, but by the end of their time on Earth, they had become giants, with species like *Quetzalcoatlus* achieving 33-foot wingspans.

DIMORPHODON

Pronunciation: dye-MORE-foe-don

Meaning: Two-form tooth

Lifestyle: Carnivore

Location: Europe (England)

Time Period: Early Jurassic (Sinemurian) 195–190 ma

Size: 4.5 ft wingspan

Dimorphodon is one of the earliest pterosaurs known. It had an unusually deep head for a pterosaur, and its jaws carried four long teeth at the front with smaller ones in the back. This tooth arrangement is suggestive of a fish-eating animal.

PTERANODON

Pronunciation: teh-RAN-oh-dawn

Meaning: Toothless wing

Lifestyle: Carnivore

Location: North America (USA, Kansas, Nebraska, Wyoming, South Dakota)

Time Period: Late Cretaceous (Santonian) 86–84 ma

Size: 20 ft wingspan

Pteranodon was a large pterosaur, with a wingspan reaching 6 meters or 20 feet. It had a long, toothless beak and a backward-pointing crest on the back of its head. We believe the crests were longer in males than in females (a case of sexual dimorphism). *Pteranodon* fossils are frequently found in marine sediments—areas that were once covered by the ocean. This has led researchers to believe that it fed on fish and spent long periods of time flying over the ocean in search of food, like the modern albatross.

THALASSODROMEUS

Pronunciation:
tha-lass-oh-DROE-mee-us

Meaning: Sea runner

Lifestyle: Carnivore

Location: South America (Brazil)

Time Period: Early Cretaceous (Albian) 110 ma

Size: 14.5 ft wingspan

In Brazil during the Cretaceous, the skies were dominated by a group of pterosaurs known as tapejarids. These were medium- to large-size pterosaurs with elaborate crests on the head. *Thalassodromeus* is a spectacular example, with a skull measuring 4.6 feet long. It gets its species name, *sethi*, from the Egyptian pharaoh Seti I, who is often depicted in a crown similar in shape to the crest of *Thalassodromeus*.

QUETZALCOATLUS

Pronunciation: ket-zahl-kwat-lus

Meaning: Aztec feathered serpent god

Lifestyle: Carnivore

Location: North America (USA, Texas)

Time Period: Late Cretaceous (Maastrichtian) 68–66 ma

Size: 33 ft wingspan

One of the largest flying creatures to have ever lived, *Quetzalcoatlus* belonged to a group of pterosaurs called **azhdarchids,** many of which reached tremendous size. *Quetzalcoatlus* was probably a ground feeder, preying on small dinosaurs, mammals, and juvenile sauropods. On the ground, it would have walked quadrupedally, supporting itself on its fingers and toes. Some paleontologists think *Quetzalcoatlus* was flightless, but others believe it could fly despite its enormous size.

Dominating the world's oceans during the Mesozoic Period were the marine reptiles: the mosasaurs, ichthyosaurs, and plesiosaurs. Just like the pterosaurs and the dinosaurs, all these marine reptiles went extinct at the end of the Cretaceous Period.

PLESIOSAURUS

Pronunciation: PLEE-zee-oh-SAWR-us

Meaning: Almost lizard

Lifestyle: Carnivore

Location: Europe (England)

Time Period: Early Jurassic (Sinemurian) 199–175 ma

Size: 11.5 ft

Evolving from land-based reptiles in the Triassic Period, plesiosaurs adapted their bodies to live life in the ocean. *Plesiosaurus* itself is typical of the group, with a streamlined body, long neck, small head, and powerful swimming paddles. It was discovered on the coast of England by Mary Anning, a young fossil hunter and paleontologist in 1823. The long necks of plesiosaurs were quite flexible from side to side, but not up and down, which means it could not lift its head far out of the water.

STENOPTERYGIUS

Pronunciation:
steh-NAWP-tehr-IHG-ee-us

Meaning: Narrow wing/fin

Lifestyle: Carnivore

Location: Europe (England, France, Germany)

Time Period: Early Jurassic (Sinemurian) 199–175 ma

Size: 11.5 ft

The ichthyosaurs evolved several million years before the dinosaurs but survived through the Mesozoic. *Stenopterygius* shows the classic, dolphin-like shape of the ichthyosaurs. Ichthyosaurs, just like dolphins, evolved from land-living animals. Their similar shape is a case of **convergent evolution,** where animals that are unrelated develop similar physical characteristics because they are living in similar environments—in this case, underwater. Many high-quality remains of *Stenopterygius* have been found, and one shows it in the process of giving birth. Unlike dinosaurs that laid eggs, ichthyosaurs gave birth to live young.

MOSASAURUS

Pronunciation: MOE-suh-SAWR-us

Meaning: Meuse River lizard

Lifestyle: Carnivore

Location: Europe (Netherlands)

Time Period: Late Cretaceous (Campanian to Maastrichtian) 82–66 ma

Size: 56 ft

The mosasaurs evolved from creatures very similar to today's monitor lizards. Often called "the *T-rex* of the ocean," *Mosasaurus* grew to enormous proportions and would have been the Cretaceous ocean's top predator. Several species of *Mosasaurus* have been described, with *Mosasaurus hoffmanii* being the largest. Mosasaurs were unique in having a second row of teeth far back in their top jaws. This allowed them to hold on to struggling prey and guide it down their throats.

We take crocodilians—crocodiles and alligators—for granted. They seem to have always been around. And that's mostly true. Crocodilians represent one of the most successful lines of animals, having been on Earth for more than 250 million years. During the Mesozoic, crocodilians of all shapes and sizes lived alongside the dinosaurs and evolved into a variety of forms, including land-based and running crocs, that no longer exist today. They also grew to enormous sizes, with some like *Sarcosuchus* of Africa and *Deinosuchus* of North America growing as big as some of the large predatory dinosaurs.

KAPROSUCHUS

Pronunciation: KAP-roh-SOOK-us

Meaning: boar crocodile

Lifestyle: Carnivore

Location: Africa (Niger)

Time Period: Late Cretaceous (Cenomanian) 95 ma

Size: 13 ft

Nicknamed "Boar Croc," *Kaprosuchus* is only known from its skull, so its full size is an estimate. Discovered in the Echkar Formation of Niger, it lived alongside other unusual crocodilians and shared its habitat with *Spinosaurus*. Its upper jaws sported three pairs of long tusk-like fangs, while its bottom jaw boasted two pairs. It appears that *Kaprosuchus* and its close relatives branched off from the main line of crocodilians and have no living relatives.

We don't often think of mammals as being around during the time of dinosaurs, but they were, in fact, quite common. Having evolved during the mid-Triassic, they remained small-but-important components of Mesozoic ecosystems. Unable to compete with the larger and more diverse dinosaurs, they remained mouse-sized until the Cretaceous when some, like *Repenomamus*, grew to the size of badgers and even feasted on baby dinosaurs.

REPENOMAMUS

Pronunciation: reh-pehn-oh-MAM-us

Meaning: Reptile mammal

Lifestyle: Carnivore

Location: Asia (China)

Time Period: Early Cretaceous (Aptian to Albian) 125–123 ma

Size: 1.5–3 ft

Throughout the Mesozoic, the dominance of dinosaurs kept mammals small, no bigger than mice or shrews. They likely fed on insects and worms, or scavenged carrion. By the early Cretaceous, some larger species had evolved. *Repenomamus* from China is one of the largest Mesozoic mammals yet discovered, and it grew to the size of a badger. Its large size meant *Repenomamus* would have a bigger impact on its ecosystem than its smaller ancestors. One fossil was found with the remains of baby dinosaurs in its stomach. Here was a mammal big enough to eat dinosaurs!

Exploring Dinosaurs

MUSEUMS

Nearly every large city has a museum with dinosaur fossils. These are usually called Science Museums or Natural History Museums, but they can go by lots of different names. Many offer special films and interactive displays involving dinosaurs. Some even offer you the chance to volunteer in dinosaur digs (fieldwork)!

For an extensive list of museums with dinosaur displays, visit https://advkeen.co/KidsDinosaursRef.

SEEING DINOSAUR FOSSILS IN THE FIELD

Visiting museums is probably the easiest way to experience dinosaur fossils, but if you're a little bit more adventurous, and your family is planning a vacation, you may be able to see dinosaur fossils in the ground where they were found!

When dinosaur fossils are still in the rocks where they were discovered, it's called "*in situ*." There are very few places where you can see dinosaur fossils in situ. Most dinosaur fossil sites are so important and valuable to science that their location is kept secret to protect them from thieves and vandals. There are, however, a few places where you can see dinosaur fossils as they were discovered.

Note that these are outdoor locations, and many of them are quite a distance from the nearest town. Always keep these safety tips in mind:

- Never go alone, but always go with an adult or an organized group.

- Check the local forecast to make sure you don't get caught in bad weather.

- Call ahead to make sure the site is open and accessible.

DINOSAUR FOSSILS IN SITU

Jurassic National Monument

125 S 600 W, Price, UT 84501
435-636-3600

The site of one of the densest collections of dinosaur bones in the United States, Jurassic National Monument features dinosaur bones in situ, as well as a full museum of mounted dinosaur skeletons.

Dinosaur National Monument

435-781-7700

Located off US Highway 40 on the border between Colorado and Utah, Dinosaur National Monument features a number of displays, including the "Wall of Bones," which contains thousands of dinosaur fossils, including the nearly complete skeleton of a juvenile *Camarasaurus*.

DINOSAUR TRACK SITES

For a detailed list of locales with dinosaur trackways (where dinosaur footprints can be seen), visit https://advkeen.co/KidsDinosaursRef

An inaccurate robot of *Dilophosaurus*

DINOSAUR ATTRACTIONS

There are several traveling shows that feature life-size robotic (animatronic) dinosaurs that roar, twitch their tails, and move around. You may also come across outside parks that feature nonmoving dinosaur sculptures, especially in the American West. Many of these can be fun and exciting, and getting the chance to see dinosaurs "fleshed out" and full-sized can be pretty awesome.

If you visit one of these attractions, keep in mind that, while they may be fun, sometimes the dinosaurs are not very accurate—that is, they don't always stick to what is known scientifically. But don't let that spoil the fun. Just be aware of it, and if you spot something you know isn't true to the science, point it out, and show what an expert you've become!

VOLUNTEER FOR A REAL DINOSAUR DIG

Many museums offer the opportunity to participate in dinosaur digs. This can be an exciting way to get "hands-on" with real dinosaur fossils in the field and to work with real paleontologists.

If you're interested in trying your hand at digging up real dinosaur fossils, check with your local museum to see if they have a program. For most museums, anyone under age 18 must be accompanied by an adult, and in many cases, they charge a fee for par-ticipating—sometimes an expensive fee, so it's best to discuss the opportunity with a parent or guardian and have them help make the arrangements.

So You Want to be a Paleontologist!

The more you learn about dinosaurs, the more you WANT to learn MORE about dinosaurs!

Becoming a paleontologist takes years of education and training. Most paleontologists have advanced degrees in several different areas, such as geology, biology, biochemistry, and mathematics. Paleontology can also include specialty areas, such as paleobotany (the study of ancient plants), paleoclimatology (the study of ancient climate systems), and paleoecology (relationships between different ancient organisms and their environments).

If you think you'd like to become a paleontologist, there's a few things you can do to get started:

Read, read, and read some more! There are hundreds of books available on dinosaurs and other ancient life-forms. Your school or public library are great resources for finding books and other types of media about dinosaurs.

Pay attention in your science classes! Even science classes that aren't about dinosaurs specifically can help your understanding about the ancient Earth and the organisms that populated it. Earth sciences like geology, ecology, and weather are all important for understanding dinosaurs and how they may have lived.

Visit your local museum! In addition to seeing dinosaur bones on display, many museums offer programs about dinosaurs. Some even offer paleontology lab experiences where you can get "hands-on" with fossils. And remember that paleontology is more than just dinosaurs . . . paleontologists study the whole range of ancient life-forms, including pterosaurs, marine reptiles, crocodiles, fish, trilobites, and more. Over time, you can even explore opportunities to volunteer at a museum and teach others what you've learned!

Start your own fossil collection! While it's not legal to collect dinosaur fossils (or fossils of any vertebrate), legally collecting fossils of invertebrates and plants is a great way to develop your field skills and learn to identify different types of ancient animals. Remember that the field of paleontology includes the study of all ancient life-forms, including invertebrates! There are a lot of books and resources out there about starting a fossil collection, and they can provide you with lots of tips and guidance. If you do start collecting fossils, keep a couple of things in mind:

- **It's against the law to collect vertebrate fossils.** Restrict your collecting to invertebrates, shells, coral, trilobites, and plants.

- **Safety first!** Never go fossil collecting alone, always have an adult with you; never go into areas that are steep or dangerous and stay away from roadways; keep an eye out for dangerous animals like some snakes and poisonous or dangerous plants.

- **Never go fossil collecting on private land** unless you receive permission from the landowner.

- **Don't collect fossils from national, state, or local parks** unless the park has rules that allow you to do so. Check first, and if you're not sure, don't collect!

Glossary

Abelisaurid: The informal name for a group of theropod (carnivorous) dinosaurs from the Cretaceous Period with deep skulls, short arms, and four-fingered hands. Includes *Carnotaurus, Majungasaurus,* and *Ekrixinatosaurus*.

Adaptation: A physical change in an organism in response to environmental, ecological, or some other stimulus (change).

Amniote: A group of vertebrates comprised of reptiles, birds, extinct parareptiles, nonavian dinosaurs, and synapsids (including mammals).

Ankylosaurs: The group of ornithischian dinosaurs with heavy body armor, including osteoderms, shoulder spikes, and (in some cases) enormous tail clubs. Examples include *Gargoyleosaurus, Pinacosaurus,* and *Ankylosaurus*.

Biped: An animal that walks on two legs.

Carnivore: An organism that primarily or exclusively eats meat.

Centrosaurines: The informal name for a subgroup of horned dinosaurs (ceratopsians) that typically display longer neck shields with elaborate ornamentation, reduced brow horns, and longer nasal horns. Examples include *Centrosaurus, Styracosaurus,* and *Diabloceratops*.

Ceratopsid: The informal name for a group of qua-drupedal, herbivorous, ornithischian dinosaurs that had rhinoceros-like bodies and large heads that bore sharp beaks, horns, and neck shields. Includes *Tricer-atops, Centrosaurus,* and *Pachyrhinosaurus*.

Chasmosaurines: The informal name for a subgroup of horned dinosaurs (ceratopsians) that typically display shorter neck shields, long brow horns, and reduced nasal horns. Examples include *Triceratops, Pentaceratops,* and *Torosaurus*.

Coelurosaur: A grouping of theropod dinosaurs that includes compsognathids, tyrannosaurs, manirap-torans, ornithomimids, and birds.

Cold blooded (see *Ectothermic*)

Dental battery: The arrangement of huge numbers of teeth in an animal that provide an effective grind-ing surface for the processing of plant material.

Dinosauria: The formal name given to the group of animals classified as dinosaurs as described by Sir Richard Owen in 1842.

Diplodocid: The informal name for a subgroup of sauropod dinosaurs characterized by extremely long necks and tails. Includes *Diplodocus, Apatosaurus,* and *Brontosaurus*.

Ectothermic (cold-blooded): The condition of an animal whose body temperature fluctuates with its surrounding temperature and gets its heat from external resources (i.e., the sun).

Endothermic (warm-blooded): The condition of an animal that maintains a constant body temperature (metabolism) and generates heat from internal processes (i.e., the processing of food).

Evolution: The process whereby an organism changes into a new genera or species through the processes of adaptation and natural selection.

Extinct: The condition whereby a genera or species of plant or animal dies off completely and ceases to exist.

Gondwana: The southern part of the supercontinent Pangea. Included what is now South America, Africa, Madagascar, India, Antarctica, and Australia.

Saurolophine: A subgroup of hadrosaur dinosaurs characterized by their lack of hollow crests in favor of smaller, solid, bony, or soft-tissue crests. Examples include *Edmontosaurus, Saurolophus,* and *Brachylophosaurus*.

Iguanodont: The informal name for a group of large-bodied ornithopod dinosaurs. Examples include *Iguanodon, Tenontosaurus, Camptosaurus,* and the hadrosaurs *Edmontosaurus, Parasaurolophus,* and *Eolambia*.

Jurassic: The middle period of the Mesozoic Era. Lasted from 199–145 million years ago.

Lambeosaurine: A subgroup of hadrosaur dinosaurs characterized by their large, hollow head crests. Examples include *Parasaurolophus, Lambeosaurus,* and *Corythosaurus*.

Laramidia: The western half of North America during the Cretaceous Period when the Western Interior Seaway split the continent in half.

Laurasia: The northern portion of the supercontinent Pangea that comprised present-day North America, Europe, and Asia.

Macronaria: A group of sauropod dinosaurs characterized by tall nasal arches and enlarged nasal openings (nostrils). Includes *Brachiosaurus, Sauroposeidon,* and *Camarasaurus*.

Marginocephalia: The group of ornithischian dinosaurs that includes the ceratopsians (the horned dinosaurs) and the pachycephalosaurs (the dome-headed dinosaurs). Examples include *Pachycephalosaurus* and *Triceratops*.

Mass extinction: The extermination of most life-forms on Earth as the result of a cataclysmic event or series of events.

Nonavian Dinosaur: All dinosaurs that are not classified as birds.

Ornithischian: One of the two major groups of dinosaurs (the other being *saurischians*). Ornithischians are characterized by the presence of beaks and a "birdlike" hip, where the pubis bone points backwards toward the tail. Includes ceratopsids (horned dinosaurs), thyreophorans (armored dinosaurs), pachycephalosaurs (dome-headed dinosaurs), and ornithopods.

Ornithopod: A subgroup of ornithischian dinosaurs. Includes the small, bipedal herbivores such as *Lesothosaurus* and *Hypsilophodon*, and the larger iguanodonts and hadrosaurs.

Osteoderm: A bony plate embedded in the skin of an animal, typically covered in keratin.

Paleontology: The study of ancient life—typically that which existed prior to the start of the Holocene epoch (11,700 years ago).

Pangea: The supercontinent that formed at the end of the Carboniferous Period and lasted into the Cretaceous Period. It was created when all of the Earth's land masses came together through the process of plate tectonics.

Predator: An animal that hunts and kills another animal for the purposes of eating it.

Prosauropod: A group of saurischian dinosaurs generally characterized by smaller size than other sauropod groups (generally less than 30 feet) and by bipedalism. Were extinct by the end of the early Triassic. Examples include *Plateosaurus, Massospondylus,* and *Anchisaurus*.

Quadruped: An animal that walks on four legs.

Raptor: The informal term used to describe dromaeosaurid dinosaurs. Raptors are typically characterized by the presence of a large killing claw on the second toes of their feet. Examples include *Velociraptor, Dakotaraptor,* and *Deinonychus*.

Reptile: The traditional grouping of animals that includes lizards, snakes, turtles, crocodilians, and dinosaurs. Now seen to encompass birds as well.

Saurischian: One of the two major groups of dinosaurs (the other being *ornithischians*). Saurischians are characterized by the presence of a "lizard-like" hip, where the pubis bone points either down or forward. Includes sauropods (such as *Brontosaurus, Diplodocus, and Argentinosaurus*), prosauropods (such as *Plateosaurus*), and theropods (*Tyrannosaurus, Therizinosaurus,* and birds).

Sauropods: Quadrupedal saurischian (lizard-hipped) dinosaurs characterized by large size (up to 30+ meters) and extremely long necks and tails. Subgroups include the diplodicids, the mamenchisaurs, and the titanosaurs, among others. Specific examples include *Brontosaurus, Mamenchisaurus*, and *Cetiosaurus*.

Sauropodomorph: A group of saurischian dinosaurs that include prosauropods and sauropods.

Scavenger: An animal that primarily or occasionally feeds off dead animals or plant materials that it did not kill.

Scute: See osteoderm.

Spine: A series of bones that make up the neck, back, hip, and tail. In dinosaurs, the spine consists of the neck or *cervical* vertebrae, the backbone or *dorsal* vertebrae, the hip or *sacral* vertebrae, and the tail or *caudal* vertebrae.

Stegosaurs: Quadrupedal ornithischian (bird-hipped) herbivorous dinosaurs characterized by short front legs, long back legs, and extensive body armor consisting of plates and spikes. Examples include *Stegosaurus, Kentrosaurus,* and *Huayangosaurus*.

Tetrapod: An animal with four limbs. Includes both living and extinct amphibians, mammals, birds, reptiles, dinosaurs, and some fish.

Theropod: A bipedal saurischian dinosaur. May be carnivorous, herbivorous, or omnivorous. Includes the tyrannosaurs, therizinosaurs, dromaeosaurs, oviraptors, ornithomimids, and birds.

Thyreophora: The group of ornithischian dinosaurs that includes the stegosaurs and the ankylosaurs. Characterized by being quadrupedal herbivores and sporting significant body armor, including plates, spikes, and tail clubs.

Titanosaur: A subgroup of sauropod dinosaurs that includes some of the largest land animals to ever live. Typically characterized by large size and (in some, but not all cases) the presence of body armor, including scutes, plates, and spikes. Examples include *Argentinosaurus* and *Saltasaurus*.

Trace Fossil: Geological records of living activity. May include footprints, trackways, coprolites, burrows, and others. Trace fossils are different from body fossils, which record parts of an animal's or plant's body.

Triassic: The middle period of the Mesozoic era. It ran from 252 to 201 million years ago.

Tyrannosaurid: The informal name for a group of carnivorous saurischian theropod dinosaurs typically characterized by fused nasal bones and premaxillary teeth (teeth at the front of the upper jaw) that are D-shaped in cross section. Examples include *Guanlong, Yutyrannus,* and *Tyrannosaurus rex*.

Vertebrate: An animal with a backbone.

Warm blooded (see *Endothermic*)

Further Exploration

RECOMMENDED READING

The Amazing World of Dinosaurs (James Kuether, ISBN 978-1-59193-645-9)

The Princeton Field Guide to Dinosaurs (Gregory S. Paul, ISBN 978-0-691-16766-4)

Fossils for Kids: Finding, Identifying, and Collecting (Dan R. Lynch, ISBN 978-1-59193-939-9)

RECOMMENDED VIEWING

SHOWS & MOVIES ABOUT OR WITH DINOSAURS AND PREHISTORIC ANIMALS

Walking With Dinosaurs (BBC/Curiosity Stream)

Walking with Prehistoric Beasts (BBC/Curiosity Stream)

Walking with Monsters: Life Before Dinosaurs (BBC/Curiosity Stream)

Prehistoric Planet (AppleTV+)

Attenborough and the Sea Dragon (PBS/Nature)

Dinosaurs Alive (Pluto TV)

Dinosaurs (Freevee)

Clash of the Dinosaurs (Discovery+)

Ancient Earth: Dinosaurs of the Frozen Continent (Curiosity Stream)

The Amazing World of Dinosaurs (Xumo)

PBS Eons (pbs.org/show/eons)

Sources

For a list of books and sources referenced in this book, see this website: https://advkeen.co/KidsDinosaursRef

About the Author

James Kuether is a freelance writer and illustrator specializing in natural history and dinosaurs. He is the author of *The Amazing World of Dinosaurs* (Adventure Publications, 2016). As an illustrator, he has contributed to more than 100 books, magazine articles, online publications, and papers. He has developed large-scale murals for the Wyoming State Museum; the Science Museum of Minnesota; the Arizona Museum of Natural History; the Hartford Children's Museum; the Museum at Dinosaur Junction; and the Dinosaur Journey Museum in Fruita, Colorado. He is a regular contributor to the Royal Tyrell Museum's education program, as well as the Canadian Encyclopedia.

About AdventureKEEN

We are an independent nature and outdoor activity publisher. Our founding dates back more than 40 years, guided then and now by our love of being in the woods and on the water, by our passion for reading and books, and by the sense of wonder and discovery made possible by spending time recreating outdoors in beautiful places. It is our mission to share that wonder and fun with our readers, especially with those who haven't yet experienced all the physical and mental health benefits that nature and outdoor activity can bring. #bewellbeoutdoors